# THE MOVEME[illegible] FACTORY WORKERS

*A Study of a New England Industrial Community*

1937-1939 and 1942

BY

CHARLES A. MYERS

AND

W. RUPERT MACLAURIN

INDUSTRIAL RELATIONS SECTION
DEPARTMENT OF ECONOMICS AND SOCIAL SCIENCE
MASSACHUSETTS INSTITUTE OF TECHNOLOGY

A PUBLICATION OF
THE TECHNOLOGY PRESS
MASSACHUSETTS INSTITUTE OF TECHNOLOGY

*NEW YORK:* JOHN WILEY & SONS, INC.
*LONDON:* CHAPMAN & HALL, LIMITED

ISBN: 0-262-63276-4 (Paperback)

PRINTED IN THE UNITED STATES OF AMERICA

# PREFACE

In this period of war, all traditional methods of conducting business need to be examined critically. Industrial relations and industrial morale have never been so important. Over the next few years we must assess various aspects of our economic structure to find inherent weaknesses and possibilities for improvement. Whether we like it or not, we are in a period of transition to a more planned society, a transition which was upon us even before the war. The war now makes it possible and necessary to analyze our industrial society in new terms and in a more critical way.

Few studies have dealt with the actual experiences of workers in our industrial towns. A composite picture of the lives of workers is extremely difficult to obtain. In 1938, therefore, the Industrial Relations Section of the Massachusetts Institute of Technology undertook this study, which analyzes the interactions of the demand and supply of factory labor in an entire industrial community.

We present here a detailed description of certain aspects of the pre-war and wartime labor market. We believe such studies are necessary to determine what main weaknesses in the operation of our labor market need to be corrected. In itself, however, the study is an attempt to give an objective picture of a local labor market without prejudging any of the issues involved. We have ventured in the concluding chapter to present some of our general impressions of the operations of this particular labor market and to raise certain questions concerning possible improvements.

In a smoothly functioning labor market, we should expect that any concerns which attempted for long to pay wages below the market rate would suffer through inability to recruit good labor or through a high turnover of their best workers. Voluntary movement toward the high-wage concerns would tend to keep wage rates for comparable jobs in line. We know, however, that labor markets do not normally operate so smoothly. There are various barriers to movement which prevent the process of equalizing wage rates for comparable jobs from taking place rapidly. This has been recognized and has led to public interference in the form of minimum wage rates.

Government regulation, however, has frequently taken place without our having acquired an intimate understanding of how the labor market actually works. If, as appears extremely probable, we are entering an extended period of much wider government planning and control, more exact information on the operations of the labor market in this country will become imperative, both in war and peace times.

This study gives a more complete description than has been available previously of the employment experience and earnings of workers in a New England industrial community from 1937 to 1942. Our attention is focused here on the extent to which workers moved voluntarily or were forced to move from one firm to another or in and out of employment during this period, and the effect of this movement.

A reader of this book who is not already aware of the unplanned, uncoordinated, and chaotic nature of our industrial life during the 1930's will certainly be struck by the haphazard and apparently wasteful methods of an American labor market. It is not the purpose of this book, however, to analyze ways of improving these methods. This will have to be the subject of special analyses of the major problems involved, with close attention paid to the substantial costs inherent in the planning process.

Some suggestions for the future are made in the concluding chapter; and, for the convenience of the reader, a chapter-by-chapter summary of the factual findings is also included. In addition, summaries are provided at the beginning of each chapter.

In undertaking this study, we have had very considerable assistance from our colleagues in the Industrial Relations Section. Professor Douglass V. Brown has been especially helpful in blocking out the original plan, and he and Professor Ralph E.

Freeman have made valuable suggestions on the final manuscript. Conrad Arensberg, Douglas McGregor, Dwight Palmer, and John Brownell helped in the early stages of the study. Gilman MacDonald of Harvard University was responsible for collecting a large part of the interview material with workers. Others who assisted earlier in the tabulation and analysis of the data were Mrs. Katherine Bessell, Mrs. Jean Enke, Mrs. Eleanor Hooper, Miss Jeanne Pearlson, and Mrs. Louise Thompson. Finally, Miss Barbara Cole and Miss Beatrice Rogers have contributed materially to the charts, tables, and processing of the manuscript, and Miss Rogers prepared the index. We are also indebted to the Committee on Social Security of the Social Science Research Council for a grant in 1940 which financed part of the field work.

CHARLES A. MYERS
W. RUPERT MACLAURIN

CAMBRIDGE, MASSACHUSETTS
*June, 1943*

## CONTENTS

# Chapter 1

## THE MOVEMENT OF LABOR AND THE LABOR MARKET

*Cotton textiles taught us a lesson. We realized that we should have been even flatter if cotton textiles had been our sole industry.*
BANK PRESIDENT.

In a country where workers are free to change jobs and to seek work of their own choice, the movement of labor should fulfill several important functions. First, it should tend to equalize wage rates and other conditions of work for comparable jobs. Second, it should serve to distribute labor where the need is greatest, geographically and industrially. Third, it should give workers an opportunity to utilize their capacities and abilities most effectively. To the extent that there is insufficient movement, these functions will be imperfectly fulfilled. On the other hand, if many workers move without these results being realized in some degree, movement is wasteful and uneconomic. Waste is also incurred if more movement takes place than is necessary to fulfill these functions.

### MOVEMENT AND EQUALIZATION OF WAGES

Theoretically, if workers could move with complete freedom between companies in a region, differences in wage rates or conditions of work for comparable jobs would induce workers to leave the poorer-paying jobs and seek the better ones. This movement would have the effect of forcing the lower-wage firms, or those with inferior working conditions, to increase their wages or otherwise make their employment more attractive, in an effort to discourage good workers from leaving and to recruit new labor. Theoretically, also, the high-wage companies would not need to make any further increases in wages until the lower-wage firms had come up to their level and the movement of workers had ceased.

In so far as this tendency toward wage equalization operates in practice, "labor turnover" serves to indicate to an employer when his wage rates or other conditions of employment are "out of line" and need to be changed. If his best workers become disgruntled enough with their present jobs to quit, or if they leave to take a better offer, this should be a signal that some changes are called for. Employers and personnel managers are increasingly recognizing the need for accurate records on labor turnover and the desirability of acting upon them. Even today, however, too few companies know the number of their workers who leave in the course of a month or a year, and for what reasons.

### Movement and Distribution of Labor

The second function of labor movement, in distributing labor where the need is greatest, follows from the first, and is particularly important in a rapidly expanding labor market. Before it became desirable to restrict competitive bidding for workers under wartime conditions, the payment of higher wages (including "overtime") meant that expanding war plants could attract a considerable number of workers from civilian industries and from "less essential" employments like the service trades, which were not able to pay as good wages. Unemployed workers and those, such as housewives, who had never worked before were also induced to take jobs in which they were most needed.

Even in more "normal" times, the unrestricted movement of workers serves to distribute labor according to geographical and industrial shifts in the demand for labor, and enables new industries and new regions to expand. The growth of the automobile industry, for example, involved substantial migration. On the other hand, in declining industries such as bituminous coal, "depressed areas" have been created and continue to exist because outward movement has been inadequate.

### Movement and the Individual Worker

From the standpoint of the individual worker, movement has a third function: to enable him to utilize his capacities and abilities most effectively. The opportunity to move from one job to another not only may help him to improve his economic position immediately, but it also broadens his occupational experience and gives him a chance to see where he fits. Knowledge of and freedom of access to different jobs are primary conditions of the equality of opportunity that is a cornerstone of our democracy. Occupational versatility also enables workers to adjust themselves more easily to fluctuations in employment. They can "dovetail" seasonal jobs and thus secure steadier employment throughout the year.

In a period of prolonged unemployment such as this country experienced in the 1930's, some turnover among the unemployed is also extremely important. Recent studies have indicated that a worker's chance of re-employment diminishes as his period of unemployment lengthens.[1] The newly unemployed worker frequently has a better chance of being rehired than one who has been out of work for some time. This development of a "hard core" of unemployment was one of the most disturbing aspects of the pre-war labor market. To the extent that unemployed workers have an opportunity to move to jobs as other workers are laid off, the hard core is reduced, although the volume of unemployment may be the same.

## Wastes of Labor Movement

It is well known, however, that the freedom of workers to move has uneconomic aspects as well. When a newly-employed worker leaves a firm, the investment represented by the cost of hiring and training him is lost, and the process must be repeated. Frequently, however, the cost of labor turnover is only partially recognized by employers, with the result that they fail to correct faulty employment and wage practices. Movement of workers is particularly wasteful if it fails to force changes in bad personnel policies.

Ideally, new workers entering the labor market should go to those jobs which are the best available at the time. Workers seeking to better themselves should take jobs which they know represent an improvement. But adequate information about all available job opportunities is frequently lacking, and workers are often misinformed about the relative advantages of one job as compared

[1] See W. S. Woytinsky, *Three Aspects of Labor Dynamics* (Washington, 1942), pp. 66–68.

with another. The schools may fail to provide effective vocational guidance to those students who decide to seek factory employment rather than continue their schooling. In the absence of a public employment service used extensively by all employers, employed workers may learn of better jobs only through hearsay or from a friend on the spot.

The result of this lack of information or actual misinformation can be much aimless wandering or "rainbow chasing" on the part of a substantial number of workers, especially during periods of rising employment. Such experiences are not only damaging to workers' morale, but also involve losses in wages between jobs and involve costs to each firm in hiring and training replacements.

When labor shortages become general under a wartime economy, the economic disadvantages of the unrestricted movement of workers may outweigh the advantages. Labor "pirating," which is simply an effort by employers to induce workers to move, is discouraged and even restricted by government agencies because of the disruption it causes in the output of war plants. The loss of a particuarly skilled worker (who has been weaned away by another employer) may cause a bottleneck in the production of a critical ordnance item and result in widespread repercussions in an interdependent war economy. Government application of "priorities" in the movement of workers to certain plants is seriously considered when there is not enough labor to go around and when the wage offered to labor fails to be a true measure of the urgency of the need in wartime.

## Labor Market Studies

Growing labor shortages and the necessity to use our supplies of labor most effectively have emphasized the need for more adequate labor market information.[2] Earlier, during the depression, discussions of ways to meet the problem of unemployment called attention to the inadequacy of data available on the supply of

[2] Extensive information on labor supply and demand is being collected monthly by the United States Employment Service in hundreds of local labor markets. This is required for intelligent planning of training programs, recruitment of new labor, allocation of war contracts, and other problems involving labor supply considerations that arise in a war economy.

labor, the nature and extent of unemployment, and other characteristics of labor markets in the United States. Increasingly, within the last six or seven years, studies of particular labor markets have filled in some of the gaps in our knowledge.[3]

Most of these studies, however, have been focused largely on the period "after the layoff" and on the transfer of unemployed workers to other jobs and regions. We now know a good deal about the movement of workers from one place to another,[4] but less about the movement between particular industries and firms. Comparatively little attention has been paid to the movement of workers within local labor markets, the reasons for movement or lack of movement, and the effects of the movement that takes place.[5]

[3] Examples are the investigations of the Philadelphia labor market made by the Industrial Research Department of the University of Pennsylvania; the studies of the effects of industrial change on particular labor markets conducted by the National Research Project of the W.P.A.; the surveys of various state labor markets sponsored by the Committee on Social Security of the Social Science Research Council in 1936; the investigations in Minneapolis and St. Paul by the Employment Stabilization Institute of the University of Minnesota; and Professor E. Wight Bakke's studies in New Haven.

[4] See, for example, John N. Webb and Albert Westfield, "Industrial Aspects of Labor Mobility," *Monthly Labor Review* (April, 1939), pp. 789–802; and H. Makower, J. Marshak, and H. W. Robinson, "Studies in the Mobility of Labour" (a series of three articles), *Oxford Economic Papers,* Nos. 1, 2 and 4 (October, 1938, pp. 83–123; May, 1939, pp. 70–97; September, 1940, pp. 29–62). The former analyzes only transfers of workers from one community in Michigan to another; the latter reports on the number of unemployed persons moving into each county from every other county in Great Britain in recent years, and on some of the factors influencing that movement.

[5] A few studies have been made of movement within particular labor markets. Among them are Gladys L. Palmer's "The Mobility of Weavers in Three Textile Centers," *Quarterly Journal of Economics,* LV (May, 1941), pp. 460–85; Anne Bezanson, Miriam Hussey, Joseph H. Willits, and Leda F. White's *Four Years of Labor Mobility: A Study of Labor Turnover in a Group of Selected Plants in Philadelphia, 1921–24* (Supplement to Vol. CXIX of the Annals of the American Academy of Political and Social Science, Philadelphia, May, 1925); and Anne Bezanson's "The Advantages of Labor Turnover," *Quarterly Journal of Economics* (May, 1928), pp. 450–64. These studies, however, do not discuss the effect of movement on wage differentials. One approach to this problem is Carrie Glasser's *Wage Differentials: The Case of the Unskilled* (New York, 1940).

Further studies of particular local markets, therefore, are necessary. The local market, rather than some broader region, seems particularly appropriate as the subject of investigation because it is here that the forces of demand for and supply of labor first interact.[6] Within a community, workers can move from job to job without changing their residence, and we should therefore expect that movement would be greater within localities than between localities, and that its characteristics and results could be observed better.

## The Present Study

A typical, small New England industrial community is the subject of our study. We were interested in determining the extent to which factory workers moved voluntarily or were forced to move from one firm to another during the period 1937–39 and again in 1942. We sought especially to discover the factors affecting that movement, the reasons why it it was not greater, and the results of the movement. Did it fulfill the functions which movement of labor should fulfill in an orderly labor market, or were considerable wastes involved?

The records of nearly 16,000 workers form the basis of this study, but primarily it concerns a smaller sample of 1,539 workers who were laid off or who moved voluntarily during the years 1937 through 1939, and on whom considerable information was available. Interviews with a group of workers in 1940 and with officials of the principal firms in the community, both during 1937–39 and in 1942, provided a background against which this movement could be interpreted.

[6] There is no generally-agreed-upon definition of the "labor market." We speak of the "American labor market," of labor markets in particular industries, and of local labor markets. The localized character of hiring and job seeking, however, suggests that a "market" where buyers and sellers of labor meet is a small geographical area. For working purposes, the U. S. Employment Service defines a labor market roughly as one within which workers can and do commute regularly from residence to jobs, without the necessity to change residence. In other words, it is the region within which a labor supply can be recruited for local needs without necessitating migration of workers and their families.

## THE COMMUNITY STUDIED

For this intensive study of labor movement, two adjacent, medium-sized Massachusetts cities were chosen. They contained a number of different industries,[7] principally plastics, metal products, paper, apparel, furniture, and shoes, and were the trading centers of a substantial farming area. They were distant enough from other important cities to form a separate and compact labor market. In 1940 their combined population was slightly over 64,000, and, according to the 1930 census, manufacturing industries accounted for over half the total employment.[8] French-Canadians, Italians and Finns were the predominant nationalities in the labor force. Wage levels were generally not high, and unionism did not become an important factor in wage determination until 1941–42.

Industrial diversification was achieved in this community after the painful experience of mill shutdowns in the 1920's and subsequent efforts to attract new firms. As in many other New England cities, the cotton textile industry in this area suffered most after World War I. Absentee owners closed the largest single mill in the mid-twenties, leaving idle the long, many-windowed brick plants characteristic of New England's textile industry. Three other textile firms, four piano case factories, a large machine tool company, and several smaller machinery firms also ceased operation.

This reduction in the number of firms produced a sharp drop in employment even before 1929, as Chart I shows. About 1934, business and civic interests made a conscious effort to attract new companies. "Cotton textiles taught us a lesson," explained a bank

[7] The city dominated by one industry is apparently not the typical industrial community in Massachusetts. A study of thirty-one Massachusetts cities and towns, made by Professor Dwight L. Palmer of the Massachusetts Institute of Technology for the National Resources Planning Board, showed that for 1938 in two-thirds of these cities no one industry employed more than 60 per cent of the factory wage-earners and in many cities the dominant industry was considerably less important than this.

[8] Table 1, Appendix B. The percentage of manufacturing employment to total employment in the 1930 census (56 per cent) was somewhat greater than the average for the state as a whole, which was 46 per cent.

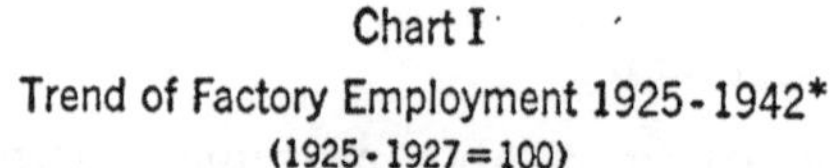


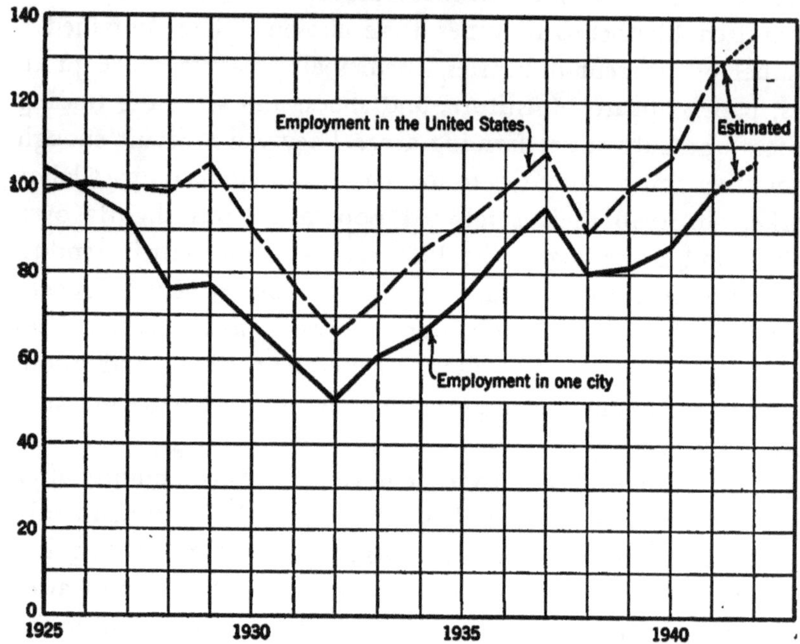


* Average annual number of wage-earners in manufacturing establishments for one city only, from the Annual Report (1941) of the Massachusetts Department of Labor and Industries. Detailed figures were not available for the other, although the trend was generally comparable. Employment data for the United States: U. S. Department of Commerce, Bureau of Foreign and Domestic Commerce, *Survey of Current Business*, 1940 Supplement, February, 1941, and February, 1942.

president who was active in this effort.[9] "We realized that we should have been even flatter if cotton textiles had been our sole

[9] Two banks in particular had a direct interest in reviving industry: they held mortgages on the buildings of two of the textile companies. The banks in at least one case provided local capital and the city continued low assessments on vacant building space during the first years of occupancy — "until the new firm could get on its feet."

But the major inducements held out to firms were the stable, diversified labor force and the advantages of locating in a small city where workers and employers would know each other as neighbors. Although lower wage levels and the absence of unions were among the factors effective in inducing at least two firms to move from large metropolitan areas, these aspects were mentioned only indirectly in the promotional publications.

industry." Although in practice the promoters welcomed "just more firms," they said they wanted new industries.

Since there was no important shoe or leather goods concern located in the community at the time, several were induced to move from other areas to take over some of the vacant plant space. Three firms, manufacturing metal products different from those already produced in the city, migrated from other New England towns. At the same time, other industries already in the area were also expanding, and by 1937 very few vacant plants remained. Recovery from 1933 to 1937 was therefore comparable with that in the United States. (Chart I.)

Subsequently, during the 1937–38 recession, employment declined slightly less than total United States factory employment.[10] Recovery in 1939 was slower than in the country as a whole because of the shutdown of a small textile mill and the partial closing of one of the large branches of a nationally owned plastics concern. Except for shortages of skilled labor in a few plants in 1937, there was a labor surplus throughout the 1937–39 period. By 1942 employment was approaching an all-time high under the impact of war production. Serious shortages of skilled workers had developed, but expanding war plants were not finding it difficult to get unskilled and semi-skilled help largely because workers were being laid off in consumers' goods industries.

Some other characteristics of the community should be mentioned. Although most of the companies were "family concerns," there was no dominant business clique. Rather, a considerable degree of individualism was found among business leaders. This was accentuated by the entrance in recent years of new types of management. The diversification effort had brought in a number of highly competitive firms, particularly shoe companies, in which

[10] According to the 1937 federal unemployment census, 11.4 per cent of the gainfully employed workers (1930) in the community studied were totally unemployed during the week of November 7–13, 1937. The corresponding percentage for the state as a whole was 13.8, and for the United States it was 11.9 per cent. *Census of Total Unemployment, Partial Unemployment, and Occupations, 1937* (Washington, 1938), Vol. II.

the management was very aggressive. And the purchase of local plants by several nationally known companies meant that management decisions were no longer governed solely by local considerations. These changes led an officer of one of the old metal products companies to say, "The town isn't what it used to be since the new element moved in. The new crowd has no business morals."

Such was the community where, in January, 1939, we began to photograph wage and personnel records. The study was confined primarily to the experience of factory workers, because the task of securing information on the employment experience of workers in the trade and service industries would have been too great for the staff and time available. Time limitations also restricted our efforts mainly to manufacturing and public utility companies that had more than fifty employees.

# Chapter 2

## AMOUNT OF MOVEMENT

*There never has been much voluntary movement in this community: Most of the workers who move are displaced workers.*
LOCAL MANAGER OF THE U. S. EMPLOYMENT SERVICE.

### SUMMARY

The major portion of this study concerns the movement of labor found in a local labor market during the pre-war years from 1937 through 1939. Individual records for nearly 16,000 wage-earners were collected from firms employing three-fourths of all factory workers in the community. In order to assess the impact of growing labor shortages on movement of workers, we returned to the community late in 1942 to re-interview the principal employers. The 1942 information is, however, more impressionistic than the 1937–39 data.

Several points stand out in the experience of factory workers in this labor market:

(1) There was a very high labor turnover. More than 70 per cent of the workers whose records were collected did not have steady employment with one firm during 1937–39. This was despite the fact that manufacturing employment in our sample of firms declined only 23 per cent from the 1937 high to the 1938 low.

(2) Less than 15 per cent of these workers actually moved between the principal factories of the community. The great majority of workers simply "disappeared" into unemployment or to other occupations, such as retail trade and truck driving. An important limitation of the study is the fact that it could say very little about the experience of these workers.

(3) In the 1937–39 period about 30 per cent of the moves between the factories in our sample were voluntary. These resulted primarily from dissatisfaction with wages, hours, or working con-

ditions, or from the definite prospect of a better job elsewhere. Approximately 70 per cent of the interfactory moves were "forced" by layoffs or discharges. In terms of total interfactory moves, differences in wage rates were not an important cause of movement.

(4) In 1942 voluntary movement was increasing but forced movements were still predominant because some firms were curtailed by materials shortages and WPB orders.

## The Method and the Data

The method followed in this study was first to discuss with the top executives of each industrial company the nature of the company's business, its wage and employment policies, and the sources of its labor supply. Permission was requested to visit the factory and have the principal operations explained. In making these visits and at subsequent interviews, we recorded our impressions of the executives, the nature of the supervision provided, working conditions, the labor relations atmosphere of the plant, and the firm's awareness of its labor turnover. We also tried to get some general information on the competitive position of the company, its past history and development, and profit and loss record.

Interviews were arranged with the mayor, the manager of the public Employment Service, bank officials, the Chamber of Commerce, the principals of the various public and parochial schools, etc. After many visits and discussions, we gradually acquired a better understanding of the general reputation and characteristics of the various companies in the community.

When we had become sufficiently well acquainted with a manufacturing concern, we asked permission to photograph by the microfilm method the wage and personnel records for all employees.[1] These records are normally regarded as highly confidential, but 37 of the 42 firms approached were willing to co-

[1] A more detailed discussion of the method and the data is found in Appendix A.

operate in making their records available. In this way we secured detailed information on the earnings and employment experience of 15,808 different workers who were employed sometime during 1937–39 in one or more of the 37 cooperating firms.

These 37 firms employed 75 per cent of all the workers in manufacturing and public utilities in the community.[2] (Table 1.) Employee records in these companies gave for most workers the date when they were first hired, weekly earnings and hours worked, dates of separation and rehiring, reason for leaving, date and place of birth, marital status, etc.[3]

Interviews with a much smaller sample of 233 workers in the summer of 1940 provided information which bridged to some extent the gaps in coverage and in company records for 1937–39. These interviews furnished information on methods of getting jobs, worker attitudes toward various firms, family work histories,

[2] Three metal products firms, which refused to make their records available, employed a total of about 1,000 workers, and their omission represents an important gap in coverage as far as the movement of labor is concerned. Later interviews with workers indicated that one of these firms, at least, was frequently involved in movement. The other omissions, one in plastics and one in apparel, are less serious.

The sample included both large and small firms, as follows:

| | |
|---|---|
| 25 to 49 employees | 3 firms |
| 50 to 99 " | 8 " |
| 100 to 249 " | 10 " |
| 250 to 499 " | 10 " |
| 500 to 749 " | 3 " |
| 750 to 999 " | 3 " |
| | 37 " |

[3] See Appendix A for a more complete description of these data. As the records were photographed over a period from January, 1939, to early 1940, they covered somewhat longer periods for the firms that were visited last. For 14 of the 37 firms, records covering only the years 1937 and 1938 were photographed; for 9 others, half of 1939 was secured in addition; and for the remaining 14, records for the full three-year period were included. No firm's records later than 1939 were secured, since the collection of this type of data was completed early in 1940.

TABLE 1

COVERAGE OF THE SAMPLE

Number of Firms and Number of Employees in Sample Compared with All Firms, Grouped by Industries (November, 1938)*

| Industry | Number of Firms | | | Number of Employees | | |
|---|---|---|---|---|---|---|
| | All | Sample | Per Cent | All | Sample | Per Cent |
| Plastics | 20 | 5 | 25 | 2,922 | 2,400 | 82 |
| Metal products | 14 | 3 | 21 | 1,989 | 750 | 38 |
| Textiles | 8 | 7 | 88 | 1,935 | 1,915 | 99 |
| Paper manufacturing | 5 | 5 | 100 | 1,723 | 1,723 | 100 |
| Apparel | 7 | 2 | 29 | 1,378 | 1,050 | 76 |
| Furniture | 12 | 2 | 17 | 912 | 535 | 59 |
| Shoes and leather products | 4 | 3 | 75 | 800 | 650 | 81 |
| Machinery | 11 | 4 | 36 | 404 | 255 | 63 |
| Public utilities | 3 | 2 | 67 | 231 | 225 | 97 |
| Converted paper products | 6 | 3 | 50 | 230 | 150 | 65 |
| Food products | 9 | 1 | 11 | 205 | 100 | 49 |
| Miscellaneous manufacturing | 21 | 0 | 0 | 267 | 0 | 0 |
| Total | 120 | 37 | 31 | 12,996 | 9,753 | 75 |

*Employment estimates, provided by the local Chamber of Commerce, are approximate only. These estimates were used in this comparison, rather than the figures from our microfilm records, in order that data for firms in the sample would be comparable with data for all industries in the community. There were no important discrepancies between the Chamber of Commerce estimates and the microfilm records.

unemployment experience, and receipt of unemployment compensation or of relief.[4]

In the late summer and fall of 1942, we re-interviewed key officials in 35 of the original 37 firms in our sample.[5] We also discussed current labor market conditions with the local manager of the United States Employment Service, with school officials, and with the personnel directors of two large war plants (not in the original sample) which figured prominently in the 1942

[4] The unemployment compensation experience of these workers was the subject of an article by the authors, "After Unemployment Benefits Are Exhausted," *Quarterly Journal of Economics*, Vol. 56, February, 1942, pp. 231–55.

[5] Two woolen textile firms had gone out of business between 1939 and 1942.

labor market. One of these had entered the community earlier in the year. No individual wage or employment records were collected for the period since 1939, and our information on movement in 1942 was, therefore, more impressionistic and less quantitative than for the 1937–39 period. Data on wage changes, current wage rates for particular jobs, and the trend of employment since 1939 were secured.

With this background on the method of the study and the nature of the data and information collected, we turn first to an examination of the amount of movement found in each period.

## Volume of Movement, 1937–39

Labor turnover in this community during 1937–39 was very high. Although the firms in our sample employed 15,808 different workers over the three years, employment in the peak month was only 9,800. Workers who had fairly continuous employment with one firm were in the minority, despite the fact that manufacturing employment in the sample of firms declined only 23 per cent from the 1937 high to the 1938 low.[6] The employment experience of the 15,808 workers whose records were photographed may be classified as follows:

| | | |
|---|---|---|
| 1. Continuously employed workers[7] . . . . | 4,563 | 29 per cent |
| 2. Workers who were employed only part of the period by any one of the 37 firms in the sample (i.e., not continuously employed) | 11,245 | 71 " " |

[6] This compares with a 25 per cent decline for the United States in the same period and a 32 per cent decline for Massachusetts. See Chart IV, Appendix B.

[7] A "continuously employed" worker was arbitrarily considered as one who had worked at least twenty weeks at the same company during each of the half-year periods covered by the records. All other workers were classified as "not continuously employed" at a particular firm. While this is necessarily only a rough classification, it does give a general idea of the relative continuity of the work force in different firms and industries. One difficulty with the method, however, is that new workers entering the labor market for the first time after 1937, and having continuous employment with the same firm thereafter, are classified as "not continuously employed." It is our impression that the number of new entrants who secured steady employment was not great.

| | | |
|---|---|---|
| *a.* Worked in two or more of the 37 firms[8] . . . . . | 1,539 | 14 per cent |
| *b.* Worked only part of period for one firm; no other firm in the 37 . . | 9,706 | 86 " " |

It is significant that, for the great majority of factory workers who were laid off or who moved for other reasons between 1937 and 1939, the chances of being rehired by another factory were small. Our 37-firm sample comprised 75 per cent of total manufacturing and public utility employment in the community, and yet only 1,539 moving workers were hired by another of the 37 firms as against the 9,706 who were not. The latter simply "disappeared" from our records.

Interviews with a very small sample of these workers who disappeared suggest that a great many of them were out of work for some time, and that the usual employment experience after leaving a factory was to find odd jobs in retail trade, domestic or personal service, restaurants, trucking, or agriculture. Some obtained other factory work in the smaller firms not included in our sample. But these interview statements could not be checked against information available from the records of the firms constituting the bulk of the manufacturing labor market. This gap in our knowledge, which appears to be inevitable without com-

[8] These workers constituted the moving group. It was the usual experience of the workers in the moving group to move between only two of the 37 firms during the period studied, although a substantial minority made more than one move, as the following summary shows:

| | | |
|---|---|---|
| Two firms . . . . . . . . . . | 1,208 | 78 per cent |
| Three firms . . . . . . . . . . | 270 | 18 " " |
| Four firms . . . . . . . . . . | 48 | 3 " " |
| Five firms . . . . . . . . . . | 13 | 1 " " |
| Total . . . . . . | 1,539 | 100 " " |

In some cases there were more moves than there were different firms involved, as a worker might return to a previous employer.

plete work-histories of every worker, constitutes a major limitation of the present study.

Consequently, this analysis of interfactory movement during 1937–39 is based primarily on the experience of the 1,539 moving workers for whom fairly complete work histories were available

TABLE 2

REASONS FOR INTERFACTORY MOVEMENT, 1937–39
(1,539 Workers)

| Types of Movement | Reasons for Leaving | Number | Per Cent |
|---|---|---|---|
| VOLUNTARY | Dissatisfaction with wages, hours, or working conditions | 52 | 2 |
| | More attractive opportunities elsewhere | 140 | 6 |
| | Family, personal, or physical reasons (largely ill health and sickness) | 96 | 4 |
| | Miscellaneous (to retire, return to school, etc.) | 6 | * |
| | Voluntary, but no further explanations given | 55 | 2 |
| | Sub-total, voluntary | 349 | 14 |
| FORCED | Discharged | 90 | 4 |
| | Laid off | 784 | 32 |
| | Sub-total, forced | 874 | 36 |
| | Reason for leaving unstated | 1,228 | 50 |
| | Total moves | 2,451 | 100 |

* Less than 1%.

because they appeared in more than one of the 37 firms. Many of these workers made more than one move during the period. The major reasons for the movement, as stated on company records, are shown in Table 2.

It will be seen from the table that reasons for leaving were unstated in the company records in half the cases. However, a separate analysis of these cases, and a comparison with interview findings indicated that they fell in approximately the same proportions of voluntary and forced movements as did the stated reasons.[9] It was our conclusion, therefore, that about 30 per cent of all the moves among the 37 firms in our sample during 1937–39 were voluntary, and about 70 per cent were forced. Most of the forced movement came from layoffs, as discharges were relatively unimportant.[10]

The company records and interviews with workers made it possible to analyze the nature of the voluntary movement in more detail than appears in Table 2.[11] Our interviews indicated, for example, that the distinction between moving "because of dis-

[9] If those movements in which little or no time elapsed between the two jobs are considered as voluntary, and those in which there was a substantial period of unemployment are regarded as forced, then about 21 per cent of the "unstated" reasons were voluntary and 79 per cent forced. On the same basis of classification, the cases in which the reasons were known would fall in the proportions of 25 and 75 per cent. Actually, 29 per cent of the movements in which the reasons were given were voluntary, and 71 per cent were forced. It seems probable, therefore, that the "unstated" reasons fall in approximately the same proportions as the stated reasons.

[10] Layoffs were the principal reason for the movement of factory workers throughout the United States at this time. The percentages of total factory labor separations due to quits, discharges, and layoffs during 1937–39 were as follows:

| *Year* | *Quits* | *Discharges* | *Layoffs* | *Total* |
|---|---|---|---|---|
| 1937 | 28% | 5% | 67% | 100% |
| 1938 | 15 | 3 | 82 | 100 |
| 1939 | 25 | 4 | 71 | 100 |

(Computed from tables in *Factory Labor Turn-over, 1931–39,* Serial No. R.1175, U. S. Bureau of Labor Statistics, 1940, pp. 4–6.) Cf. W. S. Woytinsky, *Three Aspects of Labor Dynamics* (Washington 1942), p. 4: ". . . after the beginning of 1930 about 75 per cent of all terminations in employment in manufacturing industries were initiated by employers."

As in the United States as a whole, the proportions of the different types of movement in this local labor market varied over the three years, 1937–39, but at no time were voluntary movements (quits) greater than forced movements. (Table 2, Appendix B.)

[11] See Table 3, Appendix B, for a more detailed breakdown of the 2,451 moves.

satisfaction" and because of "more attractive opportunities elsewhere" was a real one.[12] Workers who left because of more attractive opportunities frequently began work within a day or two at the new firm. Nearly half these moves were, in fact, to a "former employer."

On the other hand, those workers who, according to the firm records, quit because of dissatisfaction with a new machine, the rate of pay, the foreman, etc., were usually out of work some time before finding a job. These workers were evidently so dissatisfied with their present employment that they were willing to give up a job although there was no immediate prospect of another. Moreover, the wage rate was considerably less important in causing this type of voluntary movement than dissatisfaction with the kind and amount of work available or with working conditions. In terms of total interfactory moves, differences in wage rates were not an important cause of movement.

## Volume of Movement, 1942

By 1942 total employment was considerably higher in this community than it had been at any time since the textile shutdowns started in the 1920's. Layoffs, however, were still the principal cause of movement in the 1942 labor market. As the local manager of the United States Employment Service said: "There never has been much voluntary movement in this community. Most of the workers who move are displaced workers."

The community's industrial diversification meant that, while certain industries, such as machinery, metal products, and tex-

[12] In some cases the reason why a worker left his job may not be stated accurately in the company records. For example, a worker may quit one firm with the excuse that he has found a better job when actually he may be leaving for some other reason. Similarly, in its records a company may enter the statement "laid off" when actually the worker was considered incompetent and was discharged. It was impossible to estimate the extent to which such inaccuracies crept into the records, but it is our impression that, where reasons for leaving were listed, they were usually correct. The records were kept for the company's own use and guidance in future re-employment, and not for public or worker inspection.

tiles, were expanding very rapidly with war business, others, such as paper, plastics, and furniture, were forced to curtail for lack of war orders and the materials with which to continue their regular production. Some were restricted directly by War Production Board orders.

For example, a firm manufacturing wooden radio cabinets laid off two-thirds of its work force of 150 when civilian radio production was stopped in the spring of 1942. Materials shortages combined with a drop in orders forced a large plastics firm to lay off more than 200 workers in 1942. The same factors caused a decline of 300 in paper manufacturing employment from the beginning of the year. There was also considerable "priority" unemployment in several small outlying towns which were within commuting distance. As late as September, 1942, therefore, this community was still regarded as a "labor surplus" area.[13]

The availability of this pool of laid-off factory workers probably reduced the amount of voluntary movement that would otherwise have occurred in a community with expanding war plants. But the worker laid off in 1942 had a much better chance of finding another factory job than he did in 1937–39. With factory employment reaching all-time highs, job opportunities were more numerous than ever before.

Voluntary movement was increasing, although it was still not large relative to layoffs. The 35 firms interviewed reported about 400 voluntary quits during the first nine months of 1942,[14] as compared to twice as many layoffs. This was in contrast to the

[13] This was according to the monthly report on labor market conditions distributed by the federal Bureau of Employment Security for the confidential use of other government agencies. In August, 1942, there were nearly 2,300 workers registered for jobs, and 800 unemployed workers were drawing unemployment compensation as a result of layoffs due to materials shortages alone.

[14] A substantial number of these workers, however took jobs in large war plants in a city 30 miles distant, and others were employed by local firms not in the sample. The number of voluntary moves between the 37 firms was probably considerably smaller.

situation in the country as a whole.[15] But some companies, particularly those with lower wages and frequently with no war work, had experienced considerable voluntary movement under wartime labor market conditions. "It's tough," explained an official of a women's shoe firm, "because defense plants are hiring more, and our people are anxious to get into work which pays better anyhow." Workers were also leaving jobs in the plastics, converted paper products, and apparel companies, which ranked with shoes as low-wage firms and had comparatively few war orders.

The quit rate[16] at a large plastics company, for example, was running about 6 per cent a month in 1942. An official of a paper products firm which had a turnover of nearly 25 per cent a month explained his predicament:

> Newly hired workers either don't come to work at all the next day or work only a few days and then make some excuse that they don't like the work, or that they have another job and quit. Of course, right now with a lot of different industries in the town they can float around from firm to firm and find a job almost any place.

Although voluntary movement was not yet great, the potentialities were greater. Early in 1942, a large machinery firm acquired a local property and advertised through the public Employment Service for job applicants. About 7,000 workers ap-

[15] Beginning in February, 1941, quits became the principal reason given for movement of factory workers in the United States. The percentages of total factory labor separations due to quits, discharges, layoffs, and (after January, 1940) to "miscellaneous separations" were:

| *Year* | *Quits* | *Discharges* | *Layoffs* | *Misc. Sep.* | *Total* |
|---|---|---|---|---|---|
| 1939 | 25% | 4% | 71% | .... | 100% |
| 1940 | 27 | 5 | 64 | 4% | 100 |
| 1941 | 51 | 6 | 34 | 9 | 100 |
| 1942 (9 mos.) | 58 | 6 | 19 | 17 | 100 |

(Computed from *Labor Turn-over in Manufacturing,* U. S. Department of Labor, Bureau of Labor Statistics, December, 1940; December, 1941; September, 1942; and *Factory Labor Turn-over, 1931–39, op. cit.,* pp. 4–6.)

[16] That is, the number of quits per 100 employees.

plied, or a total equal to probably one-fourth the community's labor force. It was estimated that 90 per cent of these workers were already employed elsewhere in the community or in other areas. Nearly every firm we interviewed reported that some of its employees had applied for work with this new company, which had a reputation for excellent wages and working conditions. Non-manufacturing wage earners, such as store clerks, janitors, garage mechanics, salesmen, waitresses, and stenographers, were also among the applicants.

The 1942 labor market, therefore, was one in which a substantial number of employed workers appeared to be eager to better themselves if the opportunities were available. Since there was not yet an acute labor shortage, and for other reasons which we shall discuss later, the amount of voluntary movement was small, as it was in 1937–39. Instead, the majority of moves in both periods were initiated by employers through layoffs.

# Chapter 3

## THE NATURE OF THE MOVEMENT

*We get a lot of workers from other plastics firms. If the other plants are laying off and we're busy, their workers apply here. And two weeks ago a lot of our people were laid off and they went to other firms.*

PLASTICS EMPLOYER.

SUMMARY

In analyzing the nature of the interfactory movement that took place, we were interested in determining the factors which affected the direction of movement. Did workers move toward the higher-wage firms, or were other influences more important? We found, in fact, that there was a slight tendency for movement to be in the direction of higher-wage firms from 1937 to 1939, and a considerably stronger tendency in 1942. Much more important as an influence, however, was the tendency for workers to move within neighborhood clusters of firms. As might be expected, the greatest total movement occurred between the seasonal industries of a neighborhood or (in 1942) from civilian to neighboring war industries.

The small "active fringe" of workers who moved voluntarily between plants during 1937–39 included mostly young, short-service workers, frequently women, who were usually low-paid and felt that they had less to lose in moving than the older, higher-paid workers. Young, short-service workers were also more frequently forced to move by layoffs and discharges than were older workers. The same was substantially true in 1942.

These patterns of movement and the characteristics of the workers who moved can best be understood against a background of the principal industries in the community.

## The Community's Industries

In the 1937–39 period, 93 per cent of the moves occurred between firms in the six most seasonal industries, which employed 63 per cent of the workers studied. These industries, in order of their seasonality, were: shoes and leather products, plastics, furniture, textiles, converted paper products, and apparel. Four of them – shoes, converted paper products, plastics, and apparel – were also the lowest-wage industries of the community.

The plastics industry, which employed more workers than any other, was extremely seasonal and very competitive. The principal products were combs, sun goggles, hair ornaments, toilet ware, toothbrushes, and inexpensive novelties of all sorts. Machine methods of production and hand operations in finishing and packing made it possible to use a considerable number of workers who had relatively little training or factory experience. The industry was therefore a source of income for a great many workers who might otherwise have found difficulty getting employment. Frequently a man and his wife and their children worked in the same firm. This was particularly true of the large French-Canadian and Italian families which were among the dominant nationality groups. Working members pooled their income to support the family adequately, for wage rates and earnings in the industry were low.

What was true of the plastics industry was true to a lesser extent of the other seasonal industries in the community. The largest shoe company manufactured women's inexpensive shoes, another smaller concern produced boys' shoes, and a third manufactured women's pocketbooks and handbags. One furniture company made a well-known line of children's furniture and baby carriages, and another manufactured wooden radio cabinets on special order.

In the textile industry, three firms manufactured woolens or worsteds, one made woolen yarn, two cotton yarn, and one cotton duck cloth. Like the other seasonal industries, the textile firms typically employed a great deal of semi-skilled and unskilled labor, since only a few operations such as spinning, weaving, and loom fixing could be considered skilled. The converted paper products industry was smaller than the others, but also quite seasonal. Of the three firms, the largest manufactured photograph frames, another produced paper displays and boxes, and the third made artificial leather products. Men's shirts were the principal product of the two apparel firms, one of which specialized in a nationally advertised line that was not sold on a price competition basis.

The other industries — metal products, machinery, paper manufacturing, and public utilities — were less seasonal and less competitive, employed relatively more skilled workers, and paid higher wages. An exception was the large metal products company, which required a considerable number of semi-skilled and unskilled workers for the manufacture of a competitive line of hardware. Employment in this firm, while not seasonal, fluctuated sharply with the 1937–38 recession, in contrast to the stability of the smaller metal products companies. The machinery firms manufactured high-priced "quality" machines, which were in great demand during the period studied. Fluctuations in employment were the result of temporary shutdowns for repairs and completion of special orders rather than of seasonal factors.

The paper-manufacturing companies sold products which were partially differentiated, and competition although keen was not "cutthroat." Employment was very stable, and the industry had the lowest hiring rate of any in the sample. The same description fits the two public utility firms, one of which was a gas and electric company and the other a street railway company.

## Neighborhood Clusters of Movement

Firms in the plastics industry were located in one part of the community, and in the immediate neighborhood were companies manufacturing apparel, converted paper products, and furniture. More than 70 per cent of the moves recorded in the sample during 1937–39 occurred between firms in these four industries. In another part of the community, the three shoe and leather products companies were situated in a large building which was a few blocks from the cotton yarn mills and next door to the largest metal products firm. As in the plastics group, the number of workers who moved among these companies was much greater than the number who left for jobs in more distant parts of the community.

These neighborhood clusters of movement are pictured in Chart II, which is a rough map showing the location of the 37 firms, and the movement between them. Firms are joined by continuous lines when there was considerable two-way movement during 1937–39, and by dotted lines when there was some movement. The absence of lines indicates negligible movement or no movement.

Distance has ordinarily been thought of as a particularly important obstacle to movement between geographical regions,[1] but little mention has been made of its importance even within a local labor market.[2] Despite the fact that over a period of years workers living in one of the two adjacent cities comprising this labor market had frequently been employed in the other, nearly 90 per cent of the moves made among the 37 firms in the 1937–39 period were between companies located in the same city.[3]

[1] See e.g., H. Makower, J. Marshak, and H. W. Robinson, "Studies in the Mobility of Labour," *Oxford Economic Papers,* Nos. 1, 2, and 4 (October, 1938, pp. 83–123; May, 1939, pp. 70–97; September, 1940, pp. 29–62). This study demonstrates statistically the importance of distance in reducing the movement of labor between regions in Great Britain.

[2] A study of Philadelphia hosiery workers in the period before 1930 found that there was "considerable concentration of residence (or workers) near places of employment," although "the industry does draw on a somewhat larger area for its personnel." Studies of individual mills showed that "hosiery workers do not always work in the mill just around the corner from their homes, but that the majority live in the northeastern section of the city which is both residential and industrial." Dorothea De Schweinitz, *How Workers Find Jobs* (1932), pp. 55–60.

[3] Although the major emphasis of the study was on movement within the labor market, the interviews in 1940 with a small sample of workers brought out the fact that 63 per cent had never worked outside the two contiguous cities. Of those who had worked outside, over a fourth were in places within a radius of twenty miles, and half were in other parts of the state or near-by sections of other New England states. Jobs in near-by cities frequently did not involve migration, because it was possible to commute by automobile or bus daily.

Chart II
Intercompany and Interindustry Movements, for 1937-39

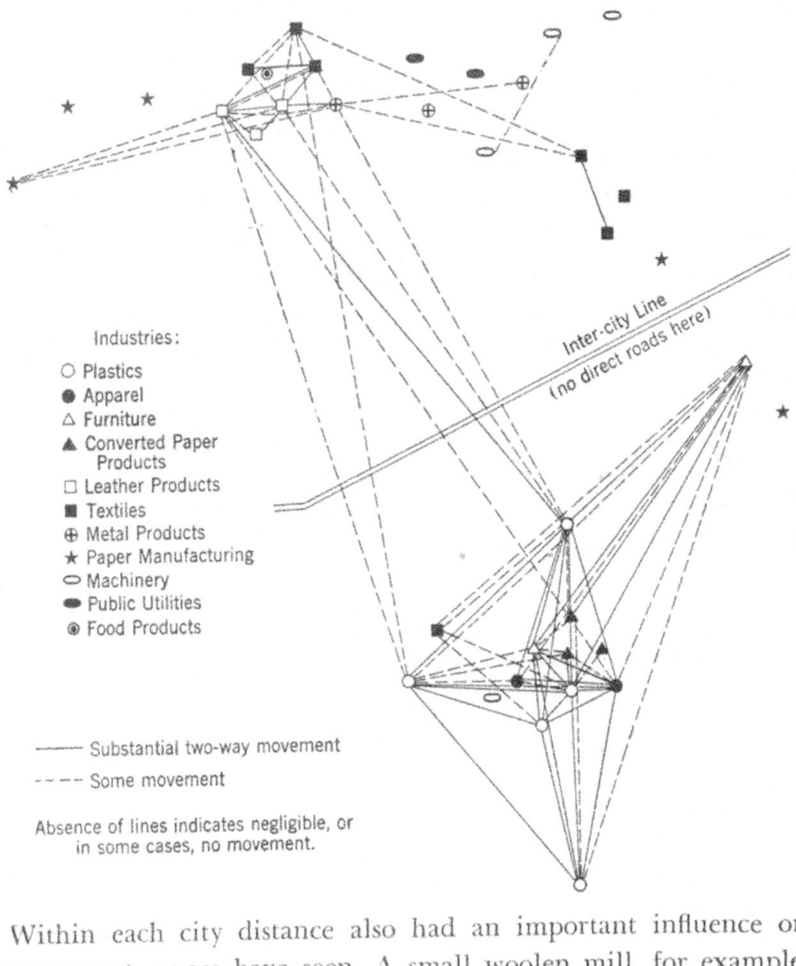

Within each city distance also had an important influence on movement, as we have seen. A small woolen mill, for example, was separated from the other textile firms, and there was little or no movement between it and the rest of the industry. On the other hand, half the movement between textiles, plastics, and apparel involved this one woolen mill, which was located in the midst of the plastics and apparel industries. (Chart II.)

In 1942, neighborhood clusters of movement were still present. For example, the largest number of job applicants at a metal products firm came from the women's shoe company next door. An analysis of the records of 62 employees hired during the summer of 1942 by a cotton textile mill showed that 43 came from firms within a quarter-mile radius. Only two had been last employed at companies located at distant parts of the community.

The attraction of higher-paying jobs in war-plants, however, was tending to break down the barriers of distance. Recently hired workers in two large metal working plants had come from widely scattered firms, not only in the community but in the surrounding region. And local firms were complaining that war plants in a large city thirty miles away were attracting local labor by the offer of higher wages.[4]

## Movement between Seasonal Industries and Firms

Table 3 shows the total intercompany movements per 100 workers for each industry. The industries are listed according to neighborhood clusters, and it can be seen that within these clusters the greatest total movement usually occurred among the seasonal industries.[5] Because busy and slack seasons did not coincide, considerable dovetailing of employment was possible.

Some examples may be cited. Workers laid off by one plastics firm following a peak period were able to get a few weeks' work in another plastics company where the busy season was not yet past. As one plastics employer explained,

[4] Movement in the other direction occurred, however, as a result of gasoline and tire rationing, and the desire of workers to find jobs nearer home if rates of pay differed by not much more than the costs of commuting. The same factors accounted for some movement within the community in 1942.

[5] An index of seasonality was computed for each industry. (See Table 5, Appendix B.) The industries were then ranked in the order of their seasonality, as follows: (1) shoes and leather products, (2) plastics, (3) furniture, (4) machinery, (5) textiles, (6) converted paper products, (7) apparel, (8) metal products, (9) public utilities, and (10) paper manufacturing. The fluctuation in the machinery industry, however, was primarily due to the completion of special orders and to shutdowns for repairs. Table 6, Appendix B, shows the peak months of employment in the neighboring seasonal industries.

TABLE 3

INTERCOMPANY MOVEMENTS PER 100 WORKERS IN EACH INDUSTRY AND BETWEEN INDUSTRIES, 1937–39*

| No. of Moves per 100 Workers from Firms in / To Firms in | Plastics | Apparel | Furniture | Converted Paper Products | Shoes and Leather Products | Textiles | Metal Products | Paper Manufacturing | Machinery | Public Utilities | Food Products | Total |
|---|---|---|---|---|---|---|---|---|---|---|---|---|
| Plastics | 17 | 3 | 1 | 1 | † | † | † | † | † | 0 | 0 | 23 |
| Apparel | 7 | 6 | 1 | † | † | † | † | † | † | 0 | 0 | 15 |
| Furniture | 9 | 2 | 3 | 2 | † | 1 | † | † | † | † | 0 | 17 |
| Converted paper products | 16 | 1 | 6 | 1 | 0 | 1 | 0 | 0 | 0 | 0 | 0 | 25 |
| Shoes and leather products | 2 | † | † | † | 6 | 3 | 2 | 1 | † | 0 | † | 14 |
| Textiles | 1 | † | † | † | 1 | 6 | † | 1 | † | † | † | 10 |
| Metal products | † | 0 | † | † | 2 | 1 | 1 | 2 | 1 | † | 0 | 7 |
| Paper manufacturing | 0 | 0 | 0 | † | † | † | † | † | 0 | † | 0 | 1 |
| Machinery | 1 | † | † | 0 | 0 | † | 1 | 1 | 2 | 0 | 0 | 5 |
| Public utilities | 0 | 0 | 0 | 0 | 0 | 0 | † | 1 | † | 1 | 0 | 2 |
| Total | 53 | 13 | 12 | 4 | 10 | 12 | 4 | 6 | 4 | 1 | † | 119 |

* The first four industries listed were located in one part of the labor market; the next three in another. The data were computed from the total work-history sheets for each industry and from the total intercompany movements in each industry, as shown in Table 7, Appendix B.

† Less than one move per 100 workers.

> We get a lot of workers from other plastics firms. If the other plants are laying off and we're busy, their workers apply here. And two weeks ago a lot of our people were laid off and they went to other firms.

Similarly, apparel workers, laid off at the end of the spring peak, could pick up a few weeks or months of work in the plastics industry before returning to their former jobs during the next busy season.

In another part of the community, seasonal variations in job opportunities and proximity of firms combined to cause considerable two-way movement between shoes and cotton textiles. Laid-off textile workers sought work in the near-by shoe firms, but usually returned to textiles when they were hiring again. Some shoe and textile workers also found employment in the more distant plastics firms, although the number who went to near-by firms and industries was comparatively greater.

In these seasonal industries, and in the few firms that were expanding during the period studied, the greatest number of job opportunities was developing. But to many of the workers who had been forced to move from their last jobs because of layoff or discharge, these were "opportunities" only in the sense that any job is better than none at all.[6] Wages in these industries were comparatively low, and the job was likely to end with the season.

By 1942, movement between seasonal industries had become less important. Workers were laid off or were quitting jobs voluntarily in such civilian goods industries as plastics, apparel, furniture, paper manufacturing, converted paper products, and shoes; and they were finding better jobs in the expanding war industries, such as metal products, machinery, and textiles. Within local neighborhoods in the community, this type of movement was substantial; but, as pointed out above, there was also increasing movement over longer distances in the community.

[6] Interviews with workers in the seasonal industries gave no evidence that they wanted to stay in those industries. Four-fifths of the persons interviewed said that they wanted full-time work, which they were not getting in the seasonal industries.

## Movement toward High-Wage Industries and Firms

Because of the importance of neighborhood location and seasonality in influencing movement, there was only a slight tendency for movement to be in the direction of high-wage industries and firms. As Table 4 shows, the amount of movement toward the higher-wage firms was very small during 1937–39. Only 102, or 4 per cent, of the 2,451 moves were from firms in the three low-wage groups to firms in the two high-wage groups. The majority of all the moves, of course, were forced, but 30 per cent were voluntary, and clearly these were not usually toward higher-wage firms.[7]

Some exceptions, however, are notable. The paper-manufacturing industry paid the highest wage rates to semi-skilled workers in 1937, and during 1937–39 it had the greatest net movement inward. That is, it attracted relatively more workers than it lost, as compared to other industries. Employment in the paper companies showed almost no cyclical recession, and wages were good. Workers employed or laid off in most other industries were glad to get a job in paper manufacturing and to hold it.

A beginner at common labor rates could earn 52½ cents an hour and $21 a week in the poorest-paying paper firm, and this was frequently better than a semi-skilled worker with experience could average in the seasonal industries. As a consequence of steady year-round employment in paper manufacturing, annual earnings of more than $1,200 were frequent, whereas in the seasonal industries this amount was unusual.

At the opposite extreme, the shoes and leather products industry paid the lowest wages and lost more workers in 1937–39, compared to those it attracted, than any other industry. Textiles and metal products, located near by, were the principal industries attracting shoe workers. Women who left the shoe companies could earn as much as $15 a week in the cotton yarn firms and at least $12 a week in the large metal products company. Wages in the largest shoe firm were frequently below $10 a week and below

[7] One-half the workers who moved voluntarily between 1937 and 1939 succeeded in improving their average hourly earnings. See Chapter 5.

TABLE 4

MOVEMENT OF WORKERS (VOLUNTARY AND FORCED) IN RELATION TO WAGE LEVELS

(Number of Moves between Groups of Firms, 1937–39) *

| From / To | Wage Level for Semi-skilled Workers† | | | | | |
|---|---|---|---|---|---|---|
| | **Very High (4 Firms)** | **Moderately High (6 Firms)** | **Medium (8 Firms)** | **Low (10 Firms)** | **Very Low (9 Firms)** | **Total (37 Firms)** |
| **Very high (Over 65¢)** | 3 | 16 | 9 | 27 | 8 | 63 |
| **Moderately high (55¢–64¢)** | 4 | 6 | 12 | 29 | 17 | 68 |
| **Medium (45¢–54¢)** | 0 | 9 | 41 | 62 | 67 | 179 |
| **Low (35¢–44¢)** | 7 | 8 | 72 | 305 | 396 | 788 |
| **Very low (Under 35¢)** | 2 | 7 | 87 | 391 | 866 | 1,353 |
| **Total** | 16 | 46 | 221 | 814 | 1,354 | 2,451 |

* A total of 1,539 workers made the 2,451 moves, 70% of which were forced and 30% voluntary.

† Information on the approximate hourly rates or, if piece rates were paid, the straight time average hourly earnings for semi-skilled workers (such as assemblers or machine-operators) was supplied by each firm. An attempt was made to choose semi-skilled operations that were fairly comparable.

25 cents an hour before the FLSA minimum became effective in October, 1938. Short-time was common. One girl, for example, was employed 20 weeks in the largest shoe firm before she quit, and her earnings averaged only $6.94 a week.[8] It is not surprising that more workers moved voluntarily from shoe firms because of "dissatisfaction" with wages or other conditions than from any other industry.

[8] A competitive shoe firm in the community (not in the sample, however) admitted at a state investigation that it had paid a "learner" $3.02 for a 23¾-hour week, but asked "whether it was better than letting the girls walk the streets." (Boston *Globe,* November 23, 1937.)

By 1942, movement toward the higher-wage firms had increased, although the amount of voluntary movement was still not large compared to forced movement, as we have seen earlier. There was, however, a more distinct relation between wage-rate levels and voluntary movement in 1942 than in 1937. All the lowest-wage firms were losing workers in 1942, whereas only four-fifths were losing workers in 1937.[9] Many low-wage employers were in the same position as a paper products manufacturer who complained: "Some firms have been sneaking our help away. They can give them a little higher price." This trend was growing, but other influences on movement still remained stronger.

## The Workers Who Moved Voluntarily

Although comparatively few workers performed the equilibrating function by moving voluntarily, it is important to consider the characteristics of these workers. Were they strikingly different from the group which was continuously employed or from the group which was forced to move by layoffs?

Table 5 compares the personnel characteristics of the workers who moved voluntarily during 1937–39 with a random sample of those workers who were continuously employed during the same period in any one of the ten firms with most voluntary movement. In other words, this provides a comparison of the most mobile group of workers with the least mobile in essentially the same firms.

The workers who moved voluntarily were a much younger group than those who remained continuously at one firm. A separate tabulation showed that they were also short-service workers. Nearly half had been employed at a firm less than ten weeks and two-thirds less than twenty weeks before moving.

Nationality and marital status differences were unimportant, but women workers were apparently more likely to move voluntarily than were men. Some of the women left their jobs voluntarily because of pregnancy, sickness in the family, and similar

[9] See Chart III, Chapter 5.

TABLE 5

PERSONNEL CHARACTERISTICS OF WORKERS WHO MOVED VOLUNTARILY, 1937–39

(Compared with a Sample of Workers Continuously Employed at Any One of the 10 Firms with Most Voluntary Movement*)

| | | Workers Moving Voluntarily | | Workers Continuously Employed in One Firm* | |
|---|---|---|---|---|---|
| | | Number | Per Cent | Number | Per Cent |
| Age | Under 25 | 171 | 49 | 3 | 9 |
| | 25–34 | 93 | 27 | 11 | 32 |
| | 35–44 | 60 | 17 | 4 | 12 |
| | 45 and over | 22 | 6 | 6 | 18 |
| | Unknown | 3 | 1 | 10 | 29 |
| | Total | 349 | 100 | 34 | 100 |
| Sex | Male | 85 | 24 | 17 | 50 |
| | Female | 264 | 76 | 17 | 50 |
| | Total | 349 | 100 | 34 | 100 |
| Marital status | Single | 136 | 39 | 11 | 32 |
| | Married | 197 | 56 | 22 | 65 |
| | Widowed, Divorced | 7 | 2 | 0 | 0 |
| | Unknown | 9 | 3 | 1 | 3 |
| | Total | 349 | 100 | 34 | 100 |
| Nationality | Native American | 56 | 16 | 11 | 32 |
| | French-Canadian | 175 | 50 | 18 | 53 |
| | Italian | 39 | 11 | 3 | 9 |
| | Irish | 21 | 6 | 0 | 0 |
| | Finnish | 7 | 2 | 2 | 6 |
| | Other | 23 | 7 | 0 | 0 |
| | Unknown | 28 | 8 | 0 | 0 |
| | Total | 349 | 100 | 34 | 100 |

* This "continuously employed" sample was selected at random, one in fifty, from the continuously employed workers in the 10 firms which had the most voluntary movement.

reasons, but these were the exceptions. The main reason for the difference perhaps lies in the fact that most of the voluntary movement originated in the seasonal industries.[10] In these industries women generally held less stable positions than men, just as younger workers were less established than older workers. They therefore had less to lose by moving in the hope of a better job. Perhaps also these women did not feel so strongly the necessity of holding on to a job at all costs, as might be the case with the principal family breadwinner. Many of the women interviewed explained their leaving particular firms with such phrases as "didn't like the foreman," "couldn't get job on the new machine," "work too hard," "they are too fussy," or "not enough pay."[11]

Workers who moved voluntarily were usually low paid. Two-thirds had been earning less than 40 cents an hour at their last job, whereas only 20 per cent of the continuously employed workers earned less than that amount. Presumably the lower-paid workers felt that they had less to lose in moving than the more established, higher-paid employees.

## Workers Who Were Forced to Move by Layoffs

None of the companies making the most extensive layoffs had a rigidly defined layoff policy. Interviews with company officials, however, made it fairly evident that a rough seniority system determined layoffs. Other things being equal, shorter-service workers were laid off before those with longer service.

10 The proportion of women in the work force was greater than 40 per cent in all of the seasonal industries except furniture, while it was 26 per cent in metal products, 13 per cent in paper manufacturing, and 11 per cent in machinery. Figures for public utilities were not readily available; but, except for the office force, the proportion of women was probably very small.

11 It is interesting to inquire into the characteristics of those voluntarily moving workers who remained with the next firm only a very short time. These workers were distinctly younger than the total group which moved voluntarily. (See Table 9, Appendix B.) There were proportionately more men, and nearly three-fifths were single persons. These facts suggest that a portion of the voluntary moving group consisted of young, unmarried male workers who desired experience and who cut themselves loose from the last job more readily than older, married workers. This very active "fringe," however, totalled less than a fifth of all workers who moved voluntarily.

TABLE 6
PERSONNEL CHARACTERISTICS OF WORKERS FORCED TO MOVE BY LAYOFFS, 1937–39
(Compared with a Sample of Workers Continuously Employed, 1937–39, at Any One of the 10 Firms with the Most Forced Movements Due to Layoffs*)

| | | Workers Laid off (in Moving Group) | | Workers Continuously Employed in One Firm* | |
|---|---|---|---|---|---|
| | | Number | Per Cent | Number | Per Cent |
| Age | Under 25 yrs. | 418 | 53 | 8 | 19 |
| | 25–34 | 224 | 29 | 18 | 44 |
| | 35–44 | 84 | 11 | 6 | 15 |
| | 45 and over | 51 | 6 | 8 | 19 |
| | Unknown | 7 | 1 | 1 | 3 |
| Sex | Male | 292 | 37 | 22 | 54 |
| | Female | 492 | 63 | 19 | 46 |
| Marital status | Single | 374 | 48 | 17 | 42 |
| | Married | 398 | 51 | 23 | 56 |
| | Widowed or Divorced | 8 | 1 | 1 | 2 |
| | Unknown | 4 | † | 0 | 0 |
| Nationality | Native American | 135 | 17 | 13 | 32 |
| | French-Canadian | 327 | 42 | 13 | 32 |
| | Italian | 174 | 22 | 10 | 24 |
| | Irish | 47 | 6 | 0 | 0 |
| | Finnish | 6 | 1 | 1 | 2 |
| | Other nationalities | 68 | 9 | 4 | 10 |
| | Unknown | 27 | 3 | 0 | 0 |

* This "continuously employed" sample was selected at random, one in fifty, from the continuously employed workers in the 10 firms which had the most forced movement due to layoffs.
† Less than 1 per cent.

It was not surprising to find, therefore, that laid-off workers in the moving group had been employed, on the average, only 24 weeks before the layoff.[12] Compared to workers continuously em-

[12] Table 11, Appendix B. Laid-off workers, however, were employed longer before being forced to move than the voluntary moving group.

ployed in the firms with the most layoffs, these laid-off workers tended to be younger than average. Table 6 shows that more than four-fifths were under 35. Once a worker had reached the age of 45, his chances of being laid off appeared to be greatly reduced.

More women were laid off than men, perhaps chiefly because the seasonal industries in which the majority of the layoffs took place had a high proportion of women among their workers. The male workers in these industries generally had the more skilled positions and were less subject to layoffs. Similarly, French-Canadians held the less skilled jobs, and this explains why proportionately more were laid off than of any other nationality. Differences in marital status between laid-off and continuously employed workers were less significant, and suggest only that workers with families may have been given a slight preference in the order of layoffs.[13]

Comparing the workers who moved voluntarily with those forced to move, we find that proportionately more male workers were laid off, although women were still in the majority. These laid-off workers were slightly younger and more likely to be single than were workers in the voluntary moving group. The sharp contrast, however, was between the moving workers as a group and the workers who were continuously employed at one firm during 1937–39. The mobile group was clearly younger, women were in the majority, and they were generally low paid.

Although detailed data on the personnel characteristics of workers were not collected in 1942, the same tendencies were evident. Officials in civilian goods industries complained that their younger workers were leaving to take better-paying war jobs, and women in particular were finding new employment opportunities in plants which formerly hired only men. The active "fringe" of workers who moved was larger, but its character had

[13] The same characteristics were even stronger among the discharged workers. (Table 12, Appendix B.) Two-thirds of the workers forced to move by discharges were single women under 25. Discharged workers also tended to have the shortest periods of service. (Table 11, Appendix B.)

not changed much betwen 1937–39 and 1942. Similarly, workers laid off by firms whose orders had dropped off or whose production or raw material supply had been curtailed were the younger, short-service workers.

# Chapter 4

## BARRIERS TO INTERFACTORY MOVEMENT

*We never take anybody who's working for another firm. We'd be sore if anybody did it to us, even though some have.*
EMPLOYMENT MANAGER OF PLASTICS FIRM.

*Most of our new employees drift in on the recommendation of friends and family members who are already at work here. Nearly everybody who applies for work has friends in the place.*
LEATHER GOODS COMPANY OFFICER.

### SUMMARY

Despite the existence of a comparative labor surplus and differences in labor requirements of the various industries, many more workers could have moved than actually did if it had not been for certain "non-competitive" practices on both the demand and supply sides of the labor market. These barriers to interfactory movement within the community were:

A. *Demand Side*
   1. The existence of a gentlemen's agreement among many of the employers not to hire labor away from each other.
   2. Other restrictive hiring practices, such as (*a*) the preference for relatives and friends of present workers, (*b*) the prejudice against hiring older employees who had worked for a considerable period of time in some of the seasonal industries, and (*c*) the preference for "unspoiled" new workers from the schools.

B. *Supply Side*
   1. The tendency of workers to seek and accept jobs in their immediate neighborhood, often through the influence of employed friends or relatives.
   2. The absence of effective vocational guidance by the schools and, during 1937–39, by the public Employment Service.
   3. The weakness of financial incentives to move, as opposed to accustomed and friendly environmental conditions or seniority rights in the job. The reluctance of many workers to risk the security of their present position by moving.

Unionism was not sufficiently widespread in this labor market until 1942 to affect movement significantly, and the unemployment compensation system was administered in such a way that laid-off workers did not tend to draw benefits in preference to seeking other jobs within the community.

## Labor Surplus and Differences in Labor Requirements

One underlying explanation of the small amount of interfactory movement, both in 1937–39 and in 1942, is the fact that the number of workers available usually exceeded the number of jobs. As we have seen, unemployment was substantial during 1937–39, although no worse than in the state and in the country as a whole. By 1942, labor shortages were growing, but they were not yet acute. The opportunities to move were probably fewer than the number of workers who wanted to move.

Because of differences in labor requirements, furthermore, it would not have been possible for substantial groups of workers to move from the low-wage to the high-wage industries. A majority of the employees in the low-wage, seasonal industries were unskilled and semi-skilled women, whereas the non-seasonal industries, if they added any workers at all, required men, and frequently those with well-developed skills.

But it is clear that there would have been more movement if it had not been for various "non-competitive" practices on both the demand and supply sides of the labor market. These practices constituted real barriers to the movement of labor within the local labor market.

## The Gentlemen's Agreement

There was relatively little active competition among employers for labor because of the "gentlemen's agreement" between a considerable number of the firms not to hire labor away from each other. Despite approaching labor shortages, the local manager of the United States Employment Service could report in 1942: "This is not a bidding market, because most of the firms are closely held or are family owned." The worker who sought to better himself by moving from one job to another was therefore distinctly handicapped by having certain job opportunities closed to him.

Examples of unwritten agreements against "stealing" or "pirating" labor during 1937–39, and even against hiring workers who apply voluntarily for work at one firm while they are still employed at another, are evident in the following interview quotations:

> *Plastics firm* — We never take anybody who's working for another firm. We'd be sore if anybody did it to us, even though some have. We've lost some good men that way, to other plastics firms, too.
>
> *Apparel company* — We don't steal labor in this town. It's more the Golden Rule than a written policy. We don't like others to do it to us, so we don't do it to them. If a person applies for work here and says he has worked elsewhere, we get on the phone and find out whether his firm still wants him. If they do, we won't take him.
>
> *Metal products firm* — A company in —— [neighboring city] has been hiring away our foundrymen, after we get them broken in, by paying higher rates than we pay. This is a policy we don't like. For our own part, we follow a policy of never hiring a man away from another company. If a person applies for work and gives as a reference another employer, we call up and find out whether he has been let go or whether the company still wants him. If they do, we don't take the man. Our experiences with foundrymen are enough to cause us to do this.

A difficulty in following this understanding was revealed by the personnel manager of a furniture firm:

> I always phone the personnel man at the firm an applicant says he's last worked for. If he wants the man, we don't hire him. Of course, some workers have discovered we do this, and now they won't say they're employed somewhere else when they apply here. We've hired a few recently and then had a call from some other firm's personnel man, dressing us down for taking their men away. We explain that it has happened unknowingly.

By 1942 the gentlemen's agreement was confined largely to plants with war work, but among these its influence in reducing voluntary movement and preventing wholesale wage changes was significant. When a new machinery firm entered the community early in 1942, rumors spread that it would pay the high starting rates which were characteristic of its plants located in other communities. Pressure was therefore brought on the company by the Chamber of Commerce, with the result that it agreed to bring its starting rate down "into line" and to avoid hiring workers already employed in other war plants. As one local machinery company executive said, the new company "is cooperating now. They realized that a wage rate war here would benefit nobody."

There was very little "pirating" of workers in the community during 1942, except from a few non-war plants.[1] One explanation was the absence of an acute labor shortage except for certain types of skilled workers. More important, however, was the fact that open competition for employed labor on a wage rate basis had long been frowned upon, and customs and traditions deeply ingrained in the community's industrial structure were not easily abandoned. Most employers felt that shortages should be met by recruiting labor from non-industrial employment, from laid-off workers, or from outside regions rather than from other factory jobs in the community.

Despite this tradition, labor shortages in 1942 forced a few firms to make modifications in the agreement. Companies in an industry that had formerly observed the agreement took a different attitude when labor shortages threatened to hold up war contracts. The president of the only shoe firm with war work said:

[1] The principal breaches in the "gentlemen's agreement" in 1942 occurred when "outside" managements entered the town. In the two cases of this that occurred, the initial hiring practices were later modified to conform to community standards. An established company that had lost workers to one of the new firms complained: "That's what happens when you get an outside firm in here. They don't care about the community. They take what they want."

There were, of course, some individualists who, as in 1937–39, did not observe the agreement in any way. They were like the manager of a woolen textile mill who said in 1942: "When I hire a worker, I don't bother to look up his past history."

> If we want girls, we can get them from the other shops because they aren't on defense work. The gentlemen's agreement doesn't apply to these shops any more. We are under obligation to get the government work out so we don't hesitate to hire workers from the other firms.

Most of the war plants would not hire any applicant who said he was actually employed elsewhere on war work, but some did not hesitate to hire without further investigation a worker who said he had quit his job. One of the woolen mills had stopped using the Employment Service as a source of new labor, because

> They will not refer a man if he is already employed on defense work somewhere else. But if you put an ad in the paper, even though it says no one should apply who is in a defense job, you will get more applicants. They will say that they are not on defense work, but everyone knows that they are and no one blames them for leaving for better jobs in our plant.

### Other Restrictive Hiring Practices

Besides the gentlemen's agreement, other hiring practices of employers accentuated the difficulties of free movement of labor. Hiring by many of the firms in the community was done by the foreman rather than through a centralized personnel department. Employment tests and job analysis were virtually non-existent. Favoritism and undue emphasis on friendship and relatives are likely to be considerably more prevalent when the foreman hires than if hiring is channelled through a central office. We found one firm in the community, a public utility, which had a fixed rule against hiring relatives. This was the only company with such a rule, and it did very little hiring during the period studied.

Prior to the war expansion, it was very difficult to get employment except through introduction by a friend or relative.[2] Only one or two of the lowest-paying companies were inclined to take anybody who turned up at the gate if there happened to be an

2 Professor Bakke found in New Haven that, next to applications received at the hiring office, "recommendations of other employees" was the most important source of new workers. This supports the unemployed worker's belief in the importance of "having someone to speak for you" in order to get a job. E. Wight Bakke, *The Unemployed Worker* (New Haven, 1940), pp. 248–50.

opening at the moment. Most firms tended to hire applicants who were recommended by other members of their family or friends already employed in the plant. The director of a local vocational school, for example, reported:

> If I send two girls to the plastics shops — one who has a mother or sister working there and one who doesn't — they will invariably take the former, even though she may not be the best girl.

Another restrictive hiring practice was the aversion of some companies to workers who had been employed for a considerable length of time in the low-wage or seasonal industries. Frequently these workers were thought to be "unreliable" or "not a high type of worker." The employment manager of a furniture firm, for instance, had developed a prejudice against plastics workers:

> Plastics people are unreliable. They come here and say they want to get settled and like it here because it's steady. Then we give them a job. But when plastics goes up they duck out and go back to plastics, where they can earn a little more per week in the busy season. So I steer clear of plastics people now. We have a higher type of employee here, anyhow.

Difficulties were also anticipated and experienced in training workers from other industries to factory methods in a different industry. As a result of these difficulties and prejudices, the higher-wage concerns frequently preferred to recruit "unspoiled" new workers from the schools. An efficient cotton yarn mill hired only "green" people because:

> Workers from other plants are too used to the methods of twenty years ago. We train most of our new workers in two months, and hire for the bottom jobs always. We get them green and fresh, right out of high school.

In a number of cases it was discovered that, under the pressure of wartime conditions, some of the poorer-paid seasonal workers made excellent recruits; but the discovery was made too late to open many opportunities to these workers during the period studied.

Employer emphasis on length of service in layoffs and rehiring was also a factor which discouraged many of the longer-service workers in the low-wage industries from competing for higher-wage openings in other plants. So long as employers rehired their laid-off or former employees, they had few openings for new workers. Furthermore, in 1942 some war plants were reluctant to hire away a long-service employee from any concern that was likely to survive the war.

There were no other important hiring preferences or restrictions, except a preference for former employees.[3] Residence and marital status apparently made very little difference to employment managers, and only a few expressed preferences for certain nationalities. A woolen mill president liked French-Canadians, regarding Finns as more "socialistic." On the other hand, the manager of a paper-manufacturing company thought that Finns were "a steady and clean-living lot," and was glad to get as many as he could.

## The Tendency toward Neighborhood Employment

The problem of explaining the special characteristics of the supply side of the labor market which clearly distinguish it from other types of markets has troubled economists for some time. One of the earlier attempts to explain the distinctive behavior of labor markets was made by J. E. Cairnes in his definition of "non-competing groups." Cairnes was impressed by the vertical barriers to the movement of workers from unskilled to skilled jobs and from the artisan class to jobs requiring professional skill.[4] While there were undoubtedly some barriers to vertical movement between unskilled and skilled jobs in this community, the most important barriers appeared to be horizontal — the lack of opportunity to move from one industry to another and the absence of effective competition among all workers for job openings.

[3] In their interviews with employment officers of fifty New Haven firms, Professor Bakke and his associates found that "nine out of ten of all firms gave first preference to their former employees if any could be found among these to do the job." Bakke, *op. cit.*, pp. 242–43.

[4] J. E. Cairnes, *Some Leading Principles of Political Economy* (London, Macmillan, 1874), p. 72.

It has already been pointed out that we found a strong tendency for clustering of movement among firms situated within a comparatively short distance of each other. This occurred despite the fact that there were sometimes considerably more promising work opportunities in other sections of the community further removed from the workers' homes or present jobs.

One explanation for this narrow range of movement is undoubtedly the fact that workers knew more about openings in near-by plants. The word got around quickly in the neighborhood when a particular company needed additional help, and workers frequently preferred to work where their friends or relatives were employed. In all our interviews, both in 1937–39 and in 1942, the influence of friends and relatives in locating and securing jobs was brought out clearly. For example, an officer of one of the leather goods companies said:

> Most of our new employees drift in on the recommendation of friends and family members who are already at work here. Nearly everybody who applies has friends in the place.

The treasurer of a small woolen yarn firm explained in 1942 how four recent women employees came to the company:

> They were all working at the plastics plant across the way. First, one applied here for a job and we hired her. Then pretty soon she brought in her sister, and then her sister brought in her chum. After that, this chum brings in her own sister.

The prevalence of this method of getting jobs is evident in Table 7, which lists the ways in which workers secured employment during 1937–40.[5]

Among the seasonal industries, a family-wage system involving

[5] Typical interview comments were: "My aunt works there and she spoke to the foreman for me." "My uncle is a boss (foreman) at the plant." "My sister works in the office." "The landlord is a boss." "Father has had a job there for ten years." "I know the boss and he offered me a job." "They always give an old hand's son a chance."

Cf. De Schweinitz, *How Workers Find Jobs*, p. 85: "Most of the (Philadelphia) hosiery workers secure their positions because a friend speaks for them in the firm where he is already employed or in a factory where he has had some previous connection."

the pooling of earnings frequently prevailed. In these industries there was a strong tendency for occupations to be transmitted from father to son. This applied not only to broad occupational groups but to particular factories, as, for example, when father and son or mother and daughter would work on similar jobs in the same plant.

TABLE 7

METHODS OF SECURING JOBS*
(1937–40)

| Method | Number | Per Cent |
|---|---|---|
| Heard of opening or secured job through relative or friend in plant | 273 | 39 |
| Applied at plant without knowledge of specific opening | 230 | 33 |
| Worked there before; was called back | 151 | 22 |
| Saw "help-wanted" ad in newspaper | 14 | 2 |
| Through public Employment Service | 3 | † |
| Through private employment agency | 1 | † |
| Other methods | 22 | 4 |
| Total | 694 | 100 |

* Based on interviews with 233 moving workers.
† Less than 1 per cent.

There were other reasons why workers preferred neighborhood employment. It was expensive and inconvenient to commute to jobs in more distant parts of the community.[6] Women workers, in particular, did not have access to private automobiles and were forced to use the bus lines, which served only parts of the community. Thus, in 1942, workers were leaving jobs which were distant from their homes to take work in expanding war plants that were located nearer.

Secondary family workers, particularly wives, preferred to work near their homes so that they could return at noon to prepare lunch for children. Many working wives kept house while sup-

[6] The total area of the two contiguous cities was approximately 58 square miles, spread out in such a way that it was nearly 10 miles from one corner to the other.

plementing the family income, and they could do so more easily if home and plant were near by.

## Absence of Effective Vocational Guidance

The importance of family and friends in directing the streams of worker movement in this community was not counteracted by other associational influences. The public high schools and the parochial schools offered practically no effective vocational guidance. During 1937–39 there was little coordination between the school system and the factories of the community. The schools were run largely on classical lines. No attempt was made to present to the students the various alternatives that they might have for work in the community. As one high school principal said: "I have a constant battle with my teachers to get them to see that they are preparing students for something else besides college."

By 1942 one vocational school was offering trade courses in machine shop work, power stitching (for the apparel industry), plastics, cabinet making, and carpentry. But students seeking work were given no help in choosing between firms, since the school avoided revealing information on wage rates, working conditions, and other aspects of particular jobs. New workers were left to find out for themselves.

The public Employment Service was also quite ineffective in directing the stream of workers entering the labor market or changing jobs between 1937 and 1939.[7] (See Table 7.) At that time the Service knew comparatively little about the various companies in the community in terms of their wage policies, general personnel practices, and their labor turnover. Moreover, the principal employers were not using the Service to any extent, part-

[7] The Employment Service was more effective in facilitating movements between declining or bankrupt firms and expanding companies, particularly in different communities in the district which it served. For example, when the failure of a doll company in a neighboring city threw about 150 persons out of work in 1939, the Service succeeded in placing a number of workers in the expanding plastics firms in the community studied. Similarly, jobs in a woolen textile company in a near-by town were found for some of the workers laid off by the closing in 1939 of one of the woolen textile mills in the sample.

ly because they had their own sources of labor supply and partly because they had not been sold on its value to them.[8]

This situation was much improved by 1942. More employers were using the Service, largely because their own methods of recruiting labor were no longer adequate. The Service now had an opportunity to demonstrate its usefulness to employers who in 1937–39 had been skeptical of its value.[9] In the meantime, its staff had learned a great deal about the various job opportunities in the town, and about the requirements of those jobs. Requests for new workers were being filled in a more satisfactory manner, and persons seeking jobs got better information than before.

It was probably still true, however, that the majority of workers considering a change or entering the labor market for the first time applied for jobs on their own rather than going through the Employment Service. One employer expressed a fairly prevalent attitude when he said: "If a man is any kind of a worker, he can get a job himself now by casting around without applying to the Service."

## The Weakness of Financial Incentives to Move

Another reason why there was not more movement in this labor market was the apathetic attitude that some workers showed toward change. There were large groups of employees, frequently in the lower-wage concerns, who had become sufficiently habitu-

[8] A few of the employers who had called on the Employment Service for workers during 1937–39 reported that they got "the floating element who were not too satisfactory." Even for skilled help, one company found that "the persons sent down are not really skilled. They say they are skilled when they aren't at all. A fellow who has been a helper to a paint sprayer will register as a paint sprayer, but not be competent." Cf. Emily H. Huntington, *Doors to Jobs* (Berkeley and Los Angeles, 1942), pp. 151–60. Only a fourth of the 350 California employers visited had used the Employment Service between 1936 and 1938, and only 10 per cent "claimed to have placed orders for any considerable number of workers."

[9] In New Haven in 1940 Professor Bakke found that "the present high estimation of the State Employment Service (on the part of employers) is a product of demonstration of value in the last two years." Bakke, *op. cit.*, pp. 249–50.

ated to their working environment so that they were not interested in moving to another concern that promised immediate payment of better wages for comparable types of work.

For example, we got the impression from several different sources that employees living in one of the large French-Canadian districts manifested less of the money-conscious, restless ambition that is characteristic of many American workers. In the fall of 1942, in one of the low-paying, non-defense factories in this district, the employees refused to work overtime. They maintained that a 40-hour week was long enough and that they wanted the rest of their time for themselves and their families. There was no evidence that these workers were not efficient during the hours when they were at work. What they wanted to protect was their way of life.

There were other instances of workers who preferred a friendlier, more informal, and less "driving" atmosphere, even though rates of pay were lower than they could get elsewhere. This was particularly true of "oldtimers" who had become accustomed to a certain shop routine and to friendly associations that they had built up through many years in one plant. These workers were not likely to leave their jobs simply for a few dollars a week more.

Non-war plants with a large proportion of such workers lost very few to war plants in 1942. One small cotton textile firm, which had no losses to other firms during 1937–39, continued to enjoy a favored position because most of its workers were older, long-service people who lived in the neighborhood around the plant. The same was true of a paper firm isolated from the others. A few young fellows went to war plants, the employment manager said, but he added:

> Many of our workers are oldtimers who wouldn't leave us even at a time like this. They own their own homes near the mill, their whole lives center around the mill, and they are satisfied to remain where they are.

These "oldtimers" were also frequently unwilling to risk the security of their present positions by moving. As we saw in the preceding chapter, workers who moved voluntarily tended to be young, short-service workers. They had less to lose by moving than did workers with longer service. The president of a furniture firm explained:

> We haven't lost a machinist, because they get steady work and they work only during the regular daytime hours. Many of them are oldtimers and they realize that if they went elsewhere they might have to take the night shift or stand for some other inconvenience.

A similar explanation for low turnover was given by the manager of a woolen textile mill:

> Many of our people would rather work forty hours a week for the paychecks they get now than have to put in a lot of overtime and sometimes work seven days a week as they would have to in the metal plant next door. Furthermore, our people are not looking just at the present; they are looking to the future too. They realize that before this war they were getting steady work and we were running 24 hours a day. So they want to hang on to a steady job and will do it so long as they do get some pay increases from time to time. Then don't forget, "Once a textile worker, always a textile worker."

### Influence of Unemployment Compensation and Unionism on Movement

The unemployment compensation system may reduce movement if the receipt of benefits causes the unemployed worker to delay in seeking work, or if he is permitted to refuse another job because it is not regarded as "suitable employment."[10] In this community, there was little evidence that workers preferred unemployment benefits to jobs, or that the approaching end of benefits prodded them into seeking work more actively. Among the group of workers interviewed there were 133 cases of benefit

[10] In the Massachusetts law the exact definition of "suitable employment" is determined by the Director of the Division of Unemployment Compensation, but he must take into account, among other things, whether the employment "is one which is located within reasonable distance of the worker's residence or place of last employment, and is one which does not involve travel expenses substantially greater than those required in his former work." Section 16 (*d*), Massachusetts Unemployment Compensation Law.

exhaustions before re-employment, and in only a few of these did the worker give the impression that he was disinterested in employment as long as benefits were paid.[11] In the majority of cases, the interviews confirmed the findings of other studies that unemployed workers want jobs and that they start looking for work as soon as laid off if they have hope of getting another job and no prospect of an early return to the last firm.[12]

When other similar jobs were available, workers were usually required to take these jobs or lose their benefit rights. Some of the workers laid off by the best-paying plastics company in 1941, for example, were reluctant to take poorer-paying jobs in other large plastics firms. When the local unemployment compensation officials threatened to disqualify them for future benefits, however, they accepted the available employment.

Unionism was also comparatively unimportant as a barrier to movement during 1937–42. The effect of widespread unionization is probably to reduce the amount of movement.[13] Work-sharing and seniority rules tie workers to particular firms, and require the re-employment of present or former employees on a full-time basis before new workers are hired. During the first part of our study, the community was largely non-union. Less than 10 per cent of the workers employed by the 37 firms belonged to outside unions.[14] Unionization had made very little difference in the

[11] A few married women workers, for example, regarded the short seasonal layoff each year as a "vacation" and felt that they were entitled to receive their unemployment benefits during this period.

[12] For a fuller discussion of benefit exhaustion, see an article by the authors, "After Unemployment Benefits Are Exhausted," in the *Quarterly Journal of Economics,* Vol. 56, February, 1942, pp. 231–55. Cf. Bakke, *op. cit.,* Chapters VIII, and IX, and p. 308.

[13] See Sumner H. Slichter, "The Impact of Social Security Legislation on Mobility and Enterprise," Papers and Proceedings of the Fifty-Second Annual Meeting of the American Economic Association, *American Economic Review* (Supplement), XXX (March, 1940), pp. 47–48. Also his *Union Policies and Industrial Management* (Washington, 1941), pp. 151–54.

[14] Three of the five paper-manufacturing companies had signed union contracts in 1937, although organization was not complete. Both furniture firms were unionized, but the smaller one not until 1939. Other union workers in the sample were weavers in one of the woolen textile firms, bus drivers in the street railway company, and the bakers in a bakery.

layoff policies of the few organized firms, because length of service had already been given considerable weight. Only in the street railway company was it fairly clear that a union-sponsored seniority rule and benefit plan had the effect of tying workers to the company and discouraging movement.

During 1941–42, twelve more firms were unionized, leaving only seventeen non-union firms in the sample.[15] There was little evidence that the introduction of union rules had any immediate effect on movement. Some of the non-war plants may have been required to lay exclusive stress on length of service, whereas in the past occasional exceptions might have been made to take family circumstances into account. But the differences were minor, and, in any event, difficult to observe when employment generally was rising.

[15] With the exception of a public utility firm, a plastics firm, and two machinery companies, all the remaining non-union firms in the group were small.

# Chapter 5

## THE EFFECT OF THE MOVEMENT OF LABOR

> *We believe we're developing a personal relationship with our employees. We have only about 300, so I know most of them and they are always free to come in here. If the foreman has treated them wrong or made a mistake, they can come to my office and I will always go to bat for them.*
>
> COMPANY PRESIDENT.

> *I quit. I was ashamed to be seen there.*
>
> WORKER, SAME FIRM.

SUMMARY

The movement of workers that took place between the principal factories in this local labor market did not distribute labor as effectively as possible and did not serve to equalize wages and working conditions in comparable jobs. Between 1937 and 1942, the low-wage firms made some increases, but these were due more to union pressure or minimum-wage orders than to voluntary movement. Moreover, the ranking of firms in the community's wage structure was largely unchanged because the high-wage firms also made increases.

Differentials between high-wage and low-wage firms were not compensated for by differences in job conditions. On the contrary, the low-wage firms usually had poor personnel policies in other respects. Officials of these firms were frequently unaware of the excessive turnover that resulted from their policies, so movement of workers was wasteful because it failed to call attention to those practices which needed to be corrected.

Enough workers moved to provide expanding firms with an adequate labor supply. There was probably also enough movement to prevent the development of a "hard core" of unemployment among the workers in the sample during 1937–39, although some workers who had been forced to move were out of work for considerable periods of time. Workers who moved voluntarily did not always find new jobs immediately, and when they did their earnings were frequently less than in their previous job. Voluntary movement was thus a disappointing experience for some workers. Those who moved between the 37 firms did gain occupational versatility. This opportunity, however, was open only to a very small proportion of the total factory labor force.

## The Effect of Movement on Low-Wage Firms

Movement of workers to better-paying companies caused some firms to raise their wages in 1937–39.[1] The president of a converted paper products firm, for example, said:

> I don't know exactly what other firms are paying, but I did have to make some increases in 1938 and 1939 to discourage transfers to other plants. There had been a general exodus before, since the apparel factories and many others could pay higher wages.

A few companies expected that the threat of movement would be sufficient to force them to make individual increases. A small machinery firm anticipated having to raise wages because:

> A new plant is going up in this city. It will require 150 men when in full production and to get them it will have to offer more pay. So we will probably have to raise our rates to keep our men. One of our men will come to me some day and say he has been offered five cents more an hour down at this other place, and I'll tell him that he can have the same if he stays where he is. That's the way it happens.

[1] Data on "over-all turnover" and "net movement" during 1937–39 were available for firms in the various wage-level groups. "Over-all turnover" measures the degree to which a firm hired a larger number of different workers during 1937–39 than were required in the peak month of employment. "Net movement" is the difference between total outward moves (both voluntary and forced) and total inward moves. Companies which paid very high or moderately high wage rates showed a relatively low "over-all turnover" and the greatest "net movement inward." Usually also these firms gave general wage increases rather than increases on "an individual basis only." They also tended to give increases earlier than the lower-wage firms. In other words, the firms which were the "wage leaders" had the lowest "over-all turnover" and greatest "net movement inward." (See Charts V and VI, Appendix B.)

A woolen textile firm followed the largest mill in making increases:

> We follow the other company on wage rates, and now our rates are about the same as theirs. Our profit and loss account didn't warrant the two 10 per cent increases in December, 1936, and April, 1937, but they did it and we had to. I was afraid we would lose workers to them if we didn't.

By 1942, more of the lower-wage plants had been forced to make wage increases to hold key workers, to reduce turnover generally, and to attract (if possible) sufficient replacements. The cotton textile mill president who, in 1939, said, "There have been no wage changes here for years," admitted in 1942 that

> I knew an increase was coming sooner or later. The general feeling among my skilled workers was uneasy at having no increase. You know how it is. The help go home Saturday and go to church and talk to their friends about what they are getting elsewhere. Then they come in Monday morning with big ideas and there is unrest in the mill.

The threat of movement was also causing some increases, as in a women's shoe firm:

> Workers will come to the foreman and say they have a better job at 80 cents an hour or some such figure, and they may be getting only 52 cents here. We may make upward adjustments and maybe raise them to 55 cents. Strangely enough, some workers stay, so we think they are calling our bluff. Some do leave, though.

These increases in 1941 and 1942 helped to raise the wage level in the low-wage firms, and to narrow somewhat the spread that existed between high- and low-wage firms in 1937. (Chart III.) By 1942, the nine "very low-wage" firms, which paid semi-skilled workers less than 35 cents an hour in 1937, remained low relative to the others, but their rates of pay for semi-skilled workers then ran between 45 and 54 cents.

Minimum wage orders by the federal Wage-Hour Administrator, and actual or threatened union organization, however, were more important than voluntary movement in causing these increases. The starting rates in plastics, apparel, and converted

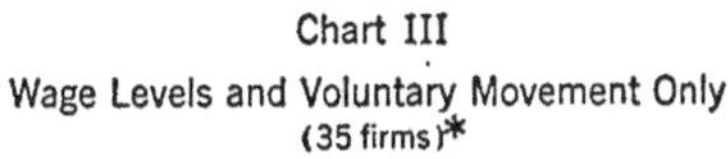


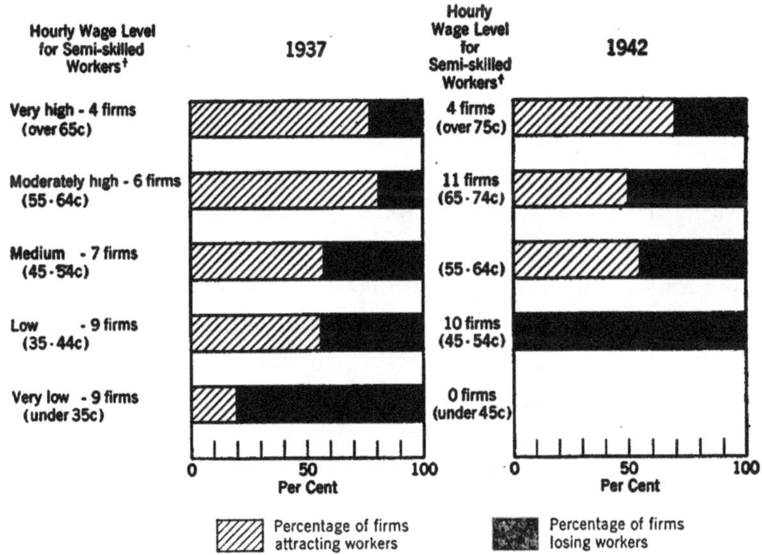


* Two of the 37 firms in the 1937–39 sample were out of business by 1942.

† Information on the approximate hourly wage rates or, if piece rates were paid, the straight time average hourly earnings for semi-skilled workers (such as assemblers or machine operators) was supplied by each firm.

paper products were increased five cents an hour during 1941 by Wage-Hour orders, and, to preserve the money differentials within the company, rates above the minimum were raised at the same time.[2] The spread of unionism to 12 firms during 1941 touched the lower-wage firms for the first time. (See Table 8.) Many of the companies in plastics, apparel, and shoes were forced to make substantial wage increases of five cents an hour, 5 per cent, or 10 per cent, and frequently there were two or more such increases. Some of the remaining non-union firms raised wages because of the desire "to keep the union out."

[2] An official of a converted paper products firm explained: "We had to take our older hands and push their rates up because they just couldn't figure out why with all their experience they should be held at the 40-cent rate."

## Increases by Higher-Wage Firms

Chart III also shows that there was a corresponding upward movement in the wage levels of many of the better-paying firms between 1937 and 1942. These firms made general wage increases in some cases through negotiations with established (or newly organized) unions, but more frequently on their own initiative. Undoubtedly the desire to attract and hold labor was a factor in these increases. The usual explanation, however, was that these firms thought their employees "were entitled" to an increase because other firms were raising wages, because the cost of living had risen, or because the firm was making money and could afford to be generous. There was no evidence that the voluntary movement of workers toward these high-wage firms had the effect of preventing further advances in wages.

Some firms had a definite wage policy which kept them ahead of the others in their industry. For example, the attitude of the largest and best-paying plastics firm (a unit of a nationally known company) was described as follows:

> The company has an important unwritten policy of paying equal to or better than the rates for comparable work in the communities in which it operates. In a community like this, where wages are relatively low, it is a policy of the company to pay rather more than the community rates, instead of just equal to them. It is good business.

This firm attracted three-fourths of all the workers who improved their hourly earnings by leaving other plastics firms.

The result of these increases by higher-wage firms was that the ranking of all firms in the wage structure of the community remained much the same from 1937 to 1942, although the spread between very high and very low-wage firms was slightly less. (Chart III.) Other than increases at the bottom of the scale, which were due more to minimum wage orders and unionization than to voluntary movement, there were only five striking changes in the relative standing of firms. Two small metal-working plants failed to make increases in line with those made generally in the community, and they were losing younger workers and trainees as a consequence.[3] A larger machinery firm likewise had not raised wages as rapidly as others, but, because of the great amount of overtime work offered, it experienced few losses of personnel. On the other hand, a large metal products firm and a converted paper products company, both of which had considerable war work, increased their wage levels by greater amounts than the others in the group. In both, the possible loss of workers was a less important explanation than the fact that the companies were making money and wanted to avoid being unionized.

## Wages in Relation to Other Job Conditions

The persistence of wage differentials for jobs requiring comparable skill and training was not due to compensating differences in working conditions or in other perquisites such as welfare plans. Generally, the companies with superior working conditions, comprehensive welfare programs for their employees, and few or no wage cuts were *also* those which paid relatively high wages. (See Table 8.) Informal practices, such as the "one happy family" atmosphere, were successful in a few cases in compensating for higher wages and holding workers, but generally the opposite was true.[4]

One of the companies studied, for example, employed three times as many workers during 1937–39 as it needed in the peak month, and lost a substantial number of workers because of dissatisfaction and better opportunities elsewhere. The industrial

[3] The director of a local vocational school was particularly disturbed about the failure of some local machine shops to pay starting rates that would attract graduates of the school. "They'll be sorry and will adjust their rates too late," he said. "Some of our employers are just short-sighted. They are thinking about next Friday, not next January. Then next January they'll want us to furnish trainees and there just won't be any."

[4] In 1937–39, the companies that boasted most about their employees being "one happy family" usually paid the lowest wages and had the highest "over-all turnover" and "net movement outward." Firms which provided the best working conditions and welfare programs usually had the lowest "over-all turnover" and the greatest "net movement inward." (See Charts VI and VII, Appendix B.)

TABLE 8

WELFARE PROGRAMS, WORKING CONDITIONS, AND WAGE CUTS IN FIRMS IN THE VARIOUS WAGE LEVEL GROUPS, 1937–39; AND UNIONIZATION, 1937–42

| Hourly Wage Level For Semi-skilled Workers | Total Firms | Welfare Programs | | | Working Conditions | | | Wage Cuts | | | Unionization (1937–42) | | |
|---|---|---|---|---|---|---|---|---|---|---|---|---|---|
| | | None | Iso-lated | Com-prehen-sive | Below Aver-age | Aver-age | Above Aver-age | Indi-vidual Changes Only | One General Cut | No Cuts | Not Union-ized | Unionized 1937–39 | Not Unionized until 1941 |
| Very high (over 65¢) | 4 | 0 | 1 | 3 | 0 | 0 | 4 | 0 | 2 | 2 | 1 | 2 | 1 |
| Moderately high (55–64¢) | 6 | 1 | 3 | 2 | 0 | 2 | 4 | 1 | 0 | 5 | 4 | 2 | 0 |
| Medium (45–54¢) | 8 | 6 | 1 | 1 | 0 | 6 | 2 | 1 | 4 | 3 | 3 | 3 | 2 |
| Low (35–44¢) | 10 | 4 | 4 | 2 | 0 | 7 | 3 | 4 | 2 | 4 | 4 | 1 | 5 |
| Very low (under 35¢) | 9 | 6 | 3 | 0 | 3 | 6 | 0 | 6 | 0 | 3 | 5 | 0 | 4 |

relations policy of this firm was summed up in the following words of the president:

> We believe we're developing a personal relationship with our employees. We have only about 300, so I know most of them and they are always free to come in here. If the foreman has treated them wrong or made a mistake, they can come to my office and I will always go to bat for them.

From interviews with a sample group of workers, some of whom had been employed by this firm, there was little evidence that the policy had worked out as described. There were few favorable comments about the company, and one worker went so far as to say, "I quit. I was ashamed to be seen there." Turnover was excessive, and many workers left, or were discharged or laid off, after one or two weeks of work.

## Wastes of Excessive Turnover

The wastes of labor movement in failing to call attention to low wages or poor personnel policies, and therefore failing to correct them, are evident in the experience of one shoe firm. Although there was more voluntary movement from the firm, in proportion to total employment, than from any other, the company's chief executive did not know how his wages compared with those in other plants:

> I don't have the faintest idea what the other shoe companies pay, but I assume that the demands of my help on me keep the wage rate level pretty equal. The boys get together and talk over the "prices" they get. Whoever gets the least, squawks. We have raised rates right along—five or six fellows in a department.
>
> I know very little about what goes on in my competitor's business. I see Mr. —— on the street, but we talk about everything else except our business affairs. He has never been in my office, and I have never been in his. If we made a wage survey, we wouldn't believe what we heard. But we probably pay about the same as the others.

In 1942 the movement away from this firm was still great, but the officials had only a general impression of how many workers left or where they went:

> We don't keep a record of where these employees go and I learn about it only indirectly. I will look at a department's production record and ask the foreman, "Hey, what's the matter with your production yesterday?" The foreman will say, "Well, Bill Jones left us. He said he had a better job lined up." I'll tell the foreman, "Well, find somebody else. See if you can't get somebody to bring in a friend." And that's the way it happens.

This case was not exceptional. Many of the other low-wage firms in leather products, plastics, and converted paper products were equally oblivious of excessive turnover, or regarded it as unavoidable and did nothing about it. They tended to justify their wage level and poor working conditions to themselves and others on the basis of inability to offer more because of the keenness of competition.[5] No analyses were made either of turnover or of the quality of workmen that they were obtaining at the wage rate or job conditions offered, nor was any desire expressed to find answers to these questions by developing more effective personnel procedures.

"You won't find any elaborate personnel department here," explained a furniture company president. "I do most of it along with my other work." "The textile industry can't afford the overhead of a personnel manager," declared the president of a textile mill with nearly 1,000 employees. His hunch may very well have been right. He had, however, made no attempt to determine what the turnover in his company was and how much might have been saved by changing some of its personnel practices.

Although excessive movement from these low-wage firms was wasteful, it was our impression that in the period studied the low-paying companies did not suffer nearly as much in inferior

[5] When asked in 1942 why he did not pay higher wages, an officer of the largest shoe company replied: "We have a low-priced commodity which requires about as much labor as a better-grade shoe, and you know a $2.00 shoe can't stand the gaff on wages that an $8.00 shoe can."

The president of a paper box firm held a similar view: "We don't get much for our stuff and we can't afford to pay as good wages as some of the other firms in town."

workmanship as might have been expected. During most of this period, the opportunity to get a job in a high-wage factory was not open to all on the basis of merit. In consequence, many very good workers got jobs in the lower-paying firms for want of any other opportunity. Once established, they stayed on indefinitely because of various non-economic considerations. This is not to say that the highest-paying firms did not have the best picking. But in view of the selection methods used, it appeared doubtful that the penalty imposed on the low-wage firms by virtue of their wage scale was as great as one might expect. It was also our impression that, because of the keenness of competition that characterized the low-wage concerns, they were as likely to provide the kind of supervision and wage incentive system that would get a hard day's work out of their employees as were the high-wage concerns.

## Movement and Distribution of Labor

Although the companies that were expanding during the period studied were, for the most part, able to recruit as many workers as they required, they probably did not succeed in getting as good a working force as could have been obtained with freer movement. Absence of vocational guidance, inadequate hiring practices, and various frictional barriers to movement that we have already discussed were responsible. Many very good workers coming out of schools secured employment in the poorer-paying, less promising industries in which they had friends and relatives. Once established in these industries, they tended to stay on, despite more attractive opportunities elsewhere.

Moreover, the workers who did move between the sample firms were not distributed as effectively as possible. In the seasonal industries, workers were able to secure steadier employment by dovetailing jobs, but in other respects they frequently failed to better their position by moving. Only half the workers who moved voluntarily during 1937–39, for example, succeeded in improving their average hourly or average weekly earnings.[6]

Table 9 shows that workers who moved because of a "better job" elsewhere were the most likely to secure higher hourly earnings. These frequently averaged 5 to 12 cents an hour more than in the last job. But in this group, as with other voluntary movements, the striking fact is that a substantial number received lower earnings in the new firm. More than a third of all voluntary moves were toward firms in which average hourly earnings proved to be no better or poorer than in the firms which the workers left.

Either these workers were misinformed about the new job, or did not count on the possibility of wage cuts, or thought of a "better job" as something other than one involving a higher wage rate. For example, an older woman left a better-paying apparel firm for another apparel company (where earnings were lower) because the latter "was not so fussy" and was willing to let an "old hand work along at her own pace." It is likely, however, that misinformation about what the new job paid was the major explanation. Voluntary movement in this labor market was therefore not very intelligent.[7]

Many of the workers who were reported as moving voluntarily did not get other jobs immediately. Table 10 shows this experience for the different groups. The data in this table suggest that

[6] Data on earnings of individual workers were available only for the 1937–39 period, and were confined to the 37 firms in the sample. Average hourly earnings were computed for the last six-months' period in the firm moved from and for the first six-months' period in the firm moved to, using the total earnings and the total hours worked during the period as they appeared on the payroll record for the employee who moved. Similarly, average weekly earnings were computed for the same periods from the totals for earnings and for weeks worked.

[7] A somewhat larger proportion of the voluntary movements for a "better job" resulted in higher hourly earnings than in higher weekly earnings (Table 9). This may suggest that some workers were attracted by higher hourly wage rates which failed to yield higher weekly earnings because of fewer hours of work per week. In view of the emphasis given among some labor groups to the wage rate rather than to the weekly paycheck, such a situation is probable.

TABLE 9

COMPARISON OF AVERAGE HOURLY AND WEEKLY EARNINGS AT THE TWO FIRMS BETWEEN WHICH VOLUNTARY MOVEMENT OCCURRED*

| Reason for Leaving | | Earnings of Next Firm as Compared to Previous Firm | | | | |
|---|---|---|---|---|---|---|
| | | Higher | No Change | Lower | Unknown | Total |
| HOURLY EARNINGS | Dissatisfied | 26 | 5 | 15 | 6 | 52 |
| | Better job | 85 | 15 | 28 | 12 | 140 |
| | Family, personal | 39 | 16 | 28 | 13 | 96 |
| | Miscellaneous | 3 | .. | 3 | .. | 6 |
| | No details | 24 | 3 | 17 | 11 | 55 |
| | Sub-total | 177 | 39 | 91 | 42 | 349 |
| WEEKLY EARNINGS | Dissatisfied | 26 | 8 | 12 | 6 | 52 |
| | Better job | 77 | 20 | 31 | 12 | 140 |
| | Family, personal | 39 | 15 | 29 | 13 | 96 |
| | Miscellaneous | 3 | .. | 3 | .. | 6 |
| | No details | 21 | 9 | 14 | 11 | 55 |
| | Sub-total | 166 | 52 | 89 | 42 | 349 |

* Last six-months' earnings at firm moved from as compared to first six-months' earnings at firm to which movement occurred.

one of the hazards of voluntary movement is the possibility that the new job may not materialize immediately. Workers who moved voluntarily because they were "dissatisfied," for example,

TABLE

MONTHS BETWEEN JOBS, 1937–39

(Classified by types of voluntary movement)

| | Types of Movement | Months between Jobs | | | | | | | | | |
|---|---|---|---|---|---|---|---|---|---|---|---|
| | | Less than one | 1–3 | 4–6 | 7–12 | 13–18 | 19–24 | 25–36 | 37–48 | Over 48 | Total |
| VOLUNTARY | Dissatisfied | 21 | 12 | 7 | 8 | 2 | 1 | 1 | 0 | 0 | 52 |
| | Better job | 115 | 11 | 6 | 4 | 2 | 1 | 1 | 0 | 0 | 140 |
| | Family, personal | 27 | 18 | 12 | 25 | 10 | 2 | 2 | 0 | 0 | 96 |
| | Miscellaneous | 0 | 1 | 0 | 3 | 2 | 0 | 0 | 0 | 0 | 6 |
| | No details | 21 | 12 | 11 | 4 | 4 | 2 | 1 | 0 | 0 | 55 |
| | Total | 184 | 54 | 36 | 44 | 20 | 6 | 5 | 0 | 0 | 349 |
| | Per cent | 53 | 15 | 10 | 13 | 6 | 2 | 1 | 0 | 0 | 100 |

ran the risk of considerable unemployment. Only two-fifths succeeded in finding new jobs within a month.[8] In short, voluntary movement was frequently a disappointing experience.

## Occupational Changes and Versatility

Occupational facts on the nature of the new job as compared to the old were generally scarce, because of the incompleteness of many company records. But the information that was available

[8] After taking another job, workers frequently moved again within a short time. Except for those who returned to a former job, more than half the workers who moved because they were specifically dissatisfied with earnings or because of a "better job" elsewhere were employed in the new firm less than six months. The interviews with a sample of workers brought out that many of these workers left their new jobs because they had failed to better themselves as they had hoped. Three-fourths of those who stayed longer than six months, however, improved their average hourly earnings. (See Table 14, Appendix B.)

indicated that workers had a somewhat better chance of getting more money by the hour or by the week if they moved to another job in the same occupation instead of changing occupations. This was simply because workers frequently had no experience in the new job, and had to start at the beginning rate.

Workers who moved to a different type of job did gain in the sense that they were becoming more versatile. Those who could work either in plastics or apparel, for instance, were better able to adjust themselves to seasonal fluctuations in employment. Furthermore, some workers were willing to accept lower earnings at the outset in order to "get out of a rut" and enter a different type of work which offered better prospects of advancement.

As an example, one woman who was interviewed had been employed in the plastics industry during the twenties, then took a beginner's job as a shirt stitcher in the smaller apparel firm in 1931. She left this firm in 1937 for a similar job in the larger apparel firm, starting at the same rate as before. Within a few months, as she became more efficient, her average hourly and weekly earnings increased, and she had steady work thereafter.

The opportunity to move to new factory jobs and to broaden one's occupational experience, however, was open to comparatively few workers during 1937–42. Only 14 per cent of the 11,200 workers who were not continuously employed during 1937–39 in one of the 37 firms in the sample worked in two or more of these firms. And only 30 per cent of the moves made by this small group of workers were voluntary. Thus, not more than 4 per cent of all the workers were able by choice to broaden their job experience in the principal firms in the community between 1937 and 1939. The 1942 labor market was one in which more workers had the chance to try new jobs, although the amount of voluntary movement was still not great. Many workers wanted to move who did not have the opportunity to do so.

## Movement and "Hard Core" Unemployment

Those workers who did not move by choice but were forced to move by layoffs or discharges during the 1937–39 period were unemployed somewhat longer between jobs than those who moved for voluntary reasons. Less than a fifth of the discharged workers and a fourth of the laid-off workers found new jobs within a month (Table 11), as compared to half the voluntary moving workers. (Table 10.) [9]

It seems probable that movement was sufficient to prevent the development of a "hard core" of unemployment among the workers in the sample. Only 5 per cent of the laid-off workers were unemployed longer than a year before finding another job. (Table 11.) This experience, of course, is confined to those workers who did find subsequent employment among the 37 firms; it does not include workers who were laid off during 1937–39 and then did

TABLE 11

MONTHS BETWEEN JOBS, 1937–39

(Classified by types of forced movement)

| Type of Forced Movement | | Months between Jobs | | | | | | | | | |
|---|---|---|---|---|---|---|---|---|---|---|---|
| | | Less than one | 1–3 | 4–7 | 7–12 | 13–18 | 19–24 | 25–36 | 37–48 | Over 48 | Total |
| Discharged | Number | 16 | 38 | 14 | 12 | 6 | 4 | 0 | 0 | 0 | 90 |
| | Per cent | 18 | 42 | 16 | 13 | 7 | 4 | 0 | 0 | 0 | 100 |
| Laid off | Number | 196 | 284 | 116 | 144 | 93 | 11 | 1 | 0 | 0 | 845 |
| | Per cent | 25 | 36 | 15 | 19 | 4 | 1 | * | 0 | 0 | 100 |
| Total | Number | 212 | 322 | 130 | 156 | 99 | 15 | 1 | 0 | 0 | 935 |

* Less than 1%.

not appear again in any of the firms' records. Interviews with a very small random sample of these workers indicated that a greater

[9] The mean average time between jobs in movements forced by layoffs was 4 months, as compared to 1.2 months in voluntary movements for a "better job." (Table 15, Appendix B.)

number were probably unemployed longer than a year.[10] Many of them subsequently found other jobs in factories not included in the sample, and in other occupations such as retail trade, trucking, and farm work. Our data, however, shed very little light on the experience of these workers.

While layoffs probably did not give rise to a great deal of long-term unemployment in 1937–39, they caused considerable hardship in many cases. This result has been analyzed in an article which appears elsewhere,[11] in which the conclusion, based on interview evidence, is that the existing duration of unemployment benefits was not adequate to take care of the majority of the unemployed. When laid-off workers found jobs again, furthermore, their earnings per hour and per week were frequently lower than in the previous job. Less than a third succeeded in finding a better-paying job.[12]

[10] For example, 40 per cent of the workers in this group who had exhausted their unemployment benefits were out of work more than a year after drawing their last benefit check, whereas only 12 per cent of those who moved among the 37 firms were unemployed for that length of time.

[11] Charles A. Myers and W. Rupert Maclaurin, "After Unemployment Benefits Are Exhausted," *Quarterly Journal of Economics,* Vol. 56, February, 1942, pp. 231–55.

[12] See Table 16, Appendix B.

# Chapter 6

## SUMMARY AND CONCLUSIONS

### Purpose and Nature of the Study

In this study of a local labor market, we have sought to answer the following questions: How much interfactory movement took place within the community? What was the nature of that movement; who were the people that moved? What were the principal barriers to movement between local firms? Did the movement of workers fulfill its functions of (*a*) equalizing wages and other conditions of work for comparable jobs, (*b*) distributing labor where the need was greatest, and (*c*) enabling workers to better themselves and to learn new occupations?

Answers to these questions were considered important because few studies of labor markets have analyzed the character and effects of interfactory movement. More attention has been given to the unemployment experience of workers, and to movement from one locality or region to another. The necessity for better understanding of local labor markets is becoming clear under wartime pressures upon the supply of labor in various occupations, and governmental efforts to direct and control the distribution of labor.

In the medium-sized Massachusetts manufacturing community which is the subject of this study, we had an opportunity to observe the operation of a local labor market, both in a period of substantial unemployment (1937–39) and in a period of growing labor shortages (1942). The community had a number of different industries, and some workers were being laid off by civilian goods industries during 1942, when others with war contracts had expanding employment. For that reason, there was not yet an acute labor shortage in the summer and fall of 1942, when we completed our investigation.

The fact that there was a labor surplus during most of this period was important. Yet in this respect, the community was not unique. By 1937, at the beginning of the period covered by our study, it had largely recovered from the Great Depression. The trend of employment during 1937–39 was comparable to that in the United States as a whole. Similarly, in 1941 and 1942, many other industrially diversified American manufacturing cities with expanding war industries were also experiencing "priority unemployment." Labor shortages were not yet general throughout the United States in the fall of 1942.

The major part of our investigation concerned the employment experience of 1,500 workers who moved between the principal manufacturing and public utility firms in the community during 1937, 1938, and 1939. Individual records were secured initially for 16,000 workers employed at some time in the three years by 37 firms whose average employment represented 75 per cent of the factory labor force. Supplementary information was obtained from interviews with company officials between 1938 and 1941, and with a small group of workers in 1940. All the firms still in business in the summer of 1942 were interviewed again to provide comparative data and information on the 1942 labor market.

An important limitation of the study is the fact that the data provided very little information on the experience of three groups of workers: (*a*) those factory workers who took non-factory jobs or were unemployed after leaving a factory, (*b*) those who remained with one employer after entering the manufacturing labor market late in 1937, 1938, or 1939, and (*c*) those who were not employed at any time during the period in the principal manufacturing firms. If complete information had been available on these workers, it is possible that our conclusions on movement would have been modified. However, such gaps in our information seem inevitable without complete work-histories of every worker in the labor market.

## Review of Findings

The principal findings of this study may be summarized under the following points:

1. Only a small proportion of the total movement of workers during 1937–39 took place between the principal factories of the community. Seventy per cent of the 16,000 workers in the sample did not have continuous employment with one firm, and only a small percentage of these (14 per cent) found jobs in another one of the 37 firms. The experience of the other 86 per cent could not be studied in detail because some of it fell outside the major manufacturing labor market. (Chapter 2.)

2. Less than 30 per cent of the moves among the 37 firms in 1937–39 were voluntary, and 70 per cent were forced by layoffs and discharges. Thus only a small group of workers were willing or able to quit their jobs because they were dissatisfied or because they hoped to "better themselves." Forced movements were still predominant in the wartime labor market of 1942. (Chapter 2.)

3. There was a strong tendency for workers to move between industries and firms located in the same neighborhood. Some movement occurred in the direction of higher-wage firms, although it was not very great. (Chapter 3.)

4. The workers who moved voluntarily were mostly young, short-service workers, frequently women, whose earnings were relatively low in the job they quit. These workers had less to lose by moving than did the older, longer-service workers who held the better-paying jobs. Forced movements were also concentrated on the young, short-service workers, since even the non-union firms gave considerable weight to length of service in making layoffs. (Chapter 3.)

5. Despite labor surpluses and differences in skill requirements between industries, many more workers could have moved than actually did, if it had not been for certain other barriers to free movement of workers within the labor market. On the demand side, there was a gentlemen's agreement among employers not to hire labor away from each other. Employers also had certain other restrictive hiring practices which limited movement to particular groups of workers. (Chapter 4.)

6. On the supply side of the labor market, there were non-competitive practices which likewise constituted barriers to move-

ment. Workers tended to seek and accept jobs within their immediate neighborhoods largely because they learned of openings or secured jobs through the influence of employed friends and relatives. This tendency was particularly strong in the absence of effective vocational guidance by the schools and (until 1941–42) by the public Employment Service. Long service and attachment to the job or firm was another factor limiting movement in response to immediate financial incentives. Unionism and unemployment compensation had little direct influence on movement in the period studied. (Chapter 4.)

7. Movement from lower-wage to higher-wage firms was largely ineffective in reducing differentials in rates for comparable jobs. Increases by the lower-wage firms between 1937 and 1942 were brought about more by minimum-wage orders and the pressure of unions than by voluntary movement away from these firms. Higher-wage firms also made increases, thus leaving the ranking of firms in the community's wage structure unchanged, for the most part. (Chapter 5.)

8. The low-wage firms generally did not compensate for their poorer rates by providing better working conditions, welfare plans, or good "informal relations." As a result, turnover was often excessive, although many employers were unaware of it and failed to correct the personnel practices that were responsible. (Chapter 5.)

9. Because of the various barriers to movement, the high-wage, expanding firms probably did not succeed in getting the best working force that could be obtained. On the other hand, there was probably sufficient movement among the workers in the sample to prevent the development of a "hard core" of unemployment during 1937–39. (Chapter 5.)

10. Movement between the principal factories was not successful in giving workers an opportunity to utilize their capacities and abilities as effectively as possible. The fact that more than a third of the voluntary moves during 1937–39 resulted in lower earnings, and frequently some unemployment, indicates that voluntary movement was not too intelligent and often disappointing

to the workers. There was some benefit from greater occupational versatility, but the opportunity to move by choice was open only to a very small percentage of the total factory labor force. Even in 1942, the opportunities to move were fewer than the number of workers who wanted to move. (Chapter 5.)

### 1937–39 and 1942 Contrasts

The characteristics and effects of movement were much the same, both in 1937–39 and in 1942. The customary ways of getting jobs and hiring workers were too strongly ingrained in the community's structure to be altered overnight by growing labor shortages. The pressure on some firms to get and hold workers late in 1942, however, had forced certain changes which were in contrast with the 1937–39 period:

1. There was a stronger tendency for workers to move from the lower-wage to higher-wage firms. All the low-wage firms were losing workers in 1942; whereas only four-fifths were losing workers in 1937.

2. The attraction of war jobs with better wages was overcoming somewhat the attachment of workers to neighborhood firms and industries.

3. The willingness of workers to move voluntarily, and hence the potential amount of voluntary movement, was great. For example, nearly a fourth of the community's labor force, most of whom were already employed, applied for jobs with a large firm which acquired a plant in the community early in 1942. This firm was known for its good wages and personnel policies.

4. Employers with war contracts observed the "gentlemen's agreement" with other war plants, but not with non-war employers. Some firms modified it further to accept any applicant who said he had quit his job in another war plant.

5. Labor shortages in particular occupations had forced employers to turn increasingly to the public Employment Service, and the Service was measuring up to its greater responsibilities.

## Some General Impressions

Any realistic study of the labor market in the 1930's is depressing because of the enormous waste involved in the persistently recurring layoffs. Of the 16,000 workers who came under our observation, over 11,000 did not work steadily for one company during the 1937–39 period. In most companies there was no such thing as a stable work force. Even in paper manufacturing, which was much the most stable manufacturing industry, nearly half the workers did not have continuous work during the three-year period, 1937–39. At the other end of the scale, in the seasonal industries, such as plastics and shoes, the proportion was much greater. Our interviews indicated that a substantial majority of these seasonal workers were eager for full-time, year-round work if they could get it. Quite obviously, therefore, factory employment opportunities were not being provided in this community anything like equal to the demand for jobs, and most of the industrial workers were directly affected.

Since the principal factories in the community could not provide these jobs, workers were forced to turn to whatever other employment opportunities they could find. Our study was able to shed very little light on the experience of these workers because the records we collected covered mainly the larger manufacturing firms. Interviews with a few of these workers indicated that when they were not unemployed they had occasional work in retail trade, restaurants, domestic service, trucking, or agriculture, as well as in the smaller factories. But these were not the kinds of employment opportunities that most workers who had once held higher-paid factory jobs wanted. Some undoubtedly sought only part-time work, but the level of earnings in the community was such that many "supplementary" family workers were willing to take as much employment as they could get to augment the income of the principal breadwinner.

We know generally that the 1930's was a frustrating period for great masses of the people. In assessing future reactions against returning to a kind of industrial society in which the threat of a layoff was so all-pervasive, we can expect that the demand for full employment will be extremely strong. This pressure is not likely to be limited to the relatively small proportion of workers who suffered very long periods of unemployment in the 1930's. Furthermore, workers who have had good jobs for the first time, as a consequence of the war program, will not be satisfied with a return to chronic unemployment.

The amount of voluntary movement in this labor market was unusually small. Barriers to movement, such as the influence of family and friends on job seeking, must be given more weight in the economists' conception of the effect of movement in equalizing wages for comparable work. The barriers found in this labor market were sufficiently great so that, except under extreme boom conditions, the tendency toward equality of efficiency earnings was not a strong operating force.[1] The gravitational process toward higher-paying jobs was very slow. It is probably not necessary that more than a small "active fringe" of workers be willing and able to move, but the evidence is clear that, during the period of our study, the movement which did occur was not too intelligent and largely failed to correct the inequities that existed in the labor market.

### Suggestions for the Future

Further equalization of wages for comparable jobs will probably be caused more by "interference" from the government through minimum wage orders, and by the spread of collective bargaining, than by any inherent tendency for equality of efficiency earnings to be brought about by the movement of labor. Nevertheless, it is desirable in the post-war world that there be as much free movement of labor as possible. The problem of reconversion and the development of new peacetime industries

[1] Further classification and analysis of the barriers to movement in other types of labor markets and for other types of workers would be helpful. For further discussion, see W. Rupert Maclaurin and Charles A. Myers, "The Movement of Factory Labor and Its Relation to Wages," *Quarterly Journal of Economics,* Vol. 57, February, 1943, pp. 241–64.

will require considerable transfers of workers between jobs, even within local labor markets. Yet it would be a mistake if this movement should be as aimless and as frustrating as it has frequently been in the past.

In a better organized labor market, the public Employment Service will play a central role. Effective utilization of the Service by both employers and workers would go a long way toward matching workers with jobs. It would also provide a wider knowledge of alternative sources of labor supply and alternative jobs than has been available through haphazard methods of hiring and seeking work. The findings of this study suggest, however, that the Employment Service will have to gear itself to more employment outlets than those in the principal factories of the community if it is to match workers with jobs effectively. Three-fifths of the 15,808 workers in our 37-firm sample drifted out of the major manufacturing labor market sometime during 1937–39, many of them to find whatever jobs they could in non-manufacturing establishments.

Use of the Employment Service is not a substitute for a carefully planned hiring policy, but it should be helpful particularly to small firms which cannot afford elaborate personnel departments. Similarly, although the Service should probably not take the place of all efforts by individual workers to find jobs, it should make unnecessary much of the haphazard job-seeking that frequently has occurred in the past. Workers already employed, but not at the job for which they are best fitted, should be encouraged to register with the Service. Experience during the present period of war labor shortages, when the Service is being used increasingly, has done a great deal to build up the necessary confidence and make techniques of placement more effective.

Better coordination between the school system and the public Employment Service is necessary also. Certainly every young boy and girl entering the labor market is entitled, either through the Employment Service or his school, to have some assessment made for him of the various job opportunities in his community. Such an assessment should comprise a reasonably complete picture of the different types of companies and the different types of jobs. It should include some understanding of the personnel policies of the companies concerned and the nature of their cyclical and seasonal layoffs. Information of this kind, if accurately collected and disseminated fairly, should be of substantial help in finding satisfactory employment and in reducing subsequent wasteful movement.

Great improvements are possible in the hiring practices of individual business concerns, with much more attention paid to aptitudes and potentialities of individual workers and considerably less attention to friendship and relatives in hiring. Many companies still hire in a surprisingly haphazard fashion, leaving the individual decision to hire and fire up to the foreman with no review by anyone else. Except in rare cases, such procedures are bound to be unsatisfactory. Centralized hiring through the personnel department tends to reduce favoritism.

Some companies in the community knew amazingly little, both about their labor turnover or what happened to workers who quit or were laid off. Far too many workers were hired and then forgotten, their dissatisfaction not appearing until they left. In post-war reconstruction, "unskilled management" will need critical examination and careful training if labor is to be employed more effectively. Management must understand the effects on the company of a low-wage policy and a high turnover. Is the policy really paying, or does the turnover and hiring cost offset the advantages of the lower wage? When most workers remain with a company only because they cannot find a job elsewhere, the company suffers substantial "unseen costs" through lack of cooperation and slow-up. These need to be assessed. Well-run clinics for small businesses which will point out some of the effects of current hiring practices can perform great service.

Employees who suffer layoffs will need help. Looking for jobs in the 1937–39 period was an extremely discouraging experience. Laid-off workers had little chance to maintain or to improve their skills during layoffs or to develop new skills. Unemployment insurance offered some financial relief, but a detailed analysis of the unemployment insurance experience of workers in this community indicated that it was by no means adequate to take care of the unemployment suffered during the period.

However, all efforts to improve the operations of the labor market by more effective use of the Employment Service and the schools, better industrial relations practices, training of "unskilled management," relief for the unemployed, etc., will not be able to correct the main weakness. Unless cyclical depressions involving large-scale unemployment, such as that of 1937–38, can be eliminated or greatly alleviated, insecurity and the threat of a layoff will continue to dominate workers' lives. Any measures short of eliminating these major cyclical layoffs will have only a palliative effect. This fact should not be lost sight of in the current boom. The task of maintaining full employment and yet preserving enough of the dynamic aspects of capitalism to provide steady material progress to higher standards of living remains enormously difficult. It is one of our major long-run challenges.

# Appendix A

## A NOTE ON METHOD AND DATA

It is a difficult task for private investigators to undertake effective labor market research. First, it is necessary to secure the cooperation of a wide variety of firms in making their wage and personnel records available. Then there is the problem of collecting this information quickly with a limited staff, and in a form that can be conveniently tabulated and analyzed.

When this study was initiated late in 1938, discussions were first held with some of the key industrialists in the community. With the cooperation and support of these persons promised, it was easier to approach other manufacturers and gain access to individual employee records, which are ordinarily regarded as quite confidential. The procedure we followed was to secure introductions from one firm to another whenever possible. The initial approach was usually made to the president of the company. In all cases we presented an official letter from The Massachusetts Institute of Technology, explaining the general purpose of our study. The response was excellent, and only five of the forty-two firms approached were unwilling to make all their records available for study.

In recent years employers in this community, as in others, had been deluged with requests of one kind or another for information, principally by government agencies. When it was explained that this particular inquiry would involve very little work on their part, and a minimum of disturbance to the office routine, company officials were more willing to cooperate fully. The microfilm process of photographing company records made rapid collection of the data possible, in contrast to the lengthy and laborious process of copying by hand. A portable photographic machine was taken from plant to plant, and hundreds of employee records, which had to be removed only briefly from company files, were photographed within a few hours. These rolls of 16 mm. film provided a permanent record from which various types of data could subsequently be transcribed with the aid of a projector, and then analyzed in more detail later.

The data secured by this method were not uniform. Some firms kept much more complete employee records than others. The list below summarizes the sort of information found in the files of the firms which kept the best employee records:

(*a*) Name, address, social security number, company clock number.

(*b*) Other personnel information, such as date and place of birth, nationality, marital status, number of dependents, education, church affiliation, relatives working in the plant, citizenship, owning or renting home.

(*c*) Previous employers, types of jobs, and rates of pay.

(*d*) Date first hired by the company.

(*e*) Subsequent employment history: department and job, transfers, base rate of pay and changes, dates of separation and rehiring.

(*f*) Hours worked and earnings in each week employed. (This includes gross earnings, deductions for social security purposes, and net earnings.)

(*g*) Reason for leaving employment, if no longer with company or if there were temporary periods of employment elsewhere.

A form was devised for use in transcribing the most important types of information from the films after all the original records had been photographed. This form is reproduced as Chart I. One of these forms was prepared for each individual wage-earner, and the workers who moved from one firm to another were then discovered by matching the forms alphabetically.

The experience of the moving group of 1,539 workers was subsequently codified, put on punch cards, and machine-tabulated. The code sheet for this analysis is shown in Chart II.

## CHART I

COMPANY: ______ S. S. No. ______ NAME: ______

ADDRESS: ______ P. R. { ______ / ______ / ______ } NATIONALITY: ______

RELIGION: ______

BIRTHPLACE: ______ DATE OF BIRTH: ______ MARITAL STATUS: ______

DATE FIRST HIRED: ______ EDUCATION: ______

RELATIVES WORKING IN PLANT: ______ DEPENDENTS: ______

PREVIOUS EMPLOYERS: ______

______

______

| Period | Date of Employment | Department | Job | No. of Weeks | Norm. W'kly Hrs. | Total Hours | Wage Rate Piece or Hour | Earnings | Reasons for Leaving | Remarks |
|---|---|---|---|---|---|---|---|---|---|---|
| 1st 6 mos. | | | | | | | | | | |
| 2d 6 mos. | | | | | | | | | | |
| Year '37 | | | | | | | | | | |
| 1st 6 mos. | | | | | | | | | | |
| 2d 6 mos. | | | | | | | | | | |
| Year '38 | | | | | | | | | | |
| 1st 6 mos. | | | | | | | | | | |
| 2d 6 mos. | | | | | | | | | | |
| Year '39 | | | | | | | | | | |

## CHART II

## CODE SHEET

**Last name and first name or initials**

| Item | | Column |
|---|---|---|
| **Company moved from** | | **(19)** |
| **Company moved to** | | **(21)** |
| **Both companies at same time** | | **(23)** |
| **Reason for leaving company moved from** | | **(27)** |
| **Weeks worked since January, 1937, at company moved from** | | **(30)** |
| **Date first hired at company moved from** | | **(33)** |
| **Months between jobs during movement** | | **(35)** |
| **Worked before in company moved to?** | | **(37)** |
| **Same or different occupation in moving?** | | **(38)** |
| **Weeks worked since moving (in company moved to) if** | **a. Still working** | **(39)** |
| **(only 1)** | **b. Disappeared** | **(42)** |
| **Reason for leaving (if disappeared)** | | **(45)** |
| **Earnings comparison:** | **a. Same occupation — voluntary** | **(48)** |
| | **b. Same " — involuntary** | **(49)** |
| | **c. Different " — voluntary** | **(50)** |
| **(only 1)** | **d. Different " — involuntary** | **(51)** |
| | **e. ?? " — voluntary** | **(52)** |
| | **f. ?? " — involuntary** | **(53)** |
| **Age when moving** | | **(54)** |
| [illegible] | | **(56)** |
| **Birthplac[illegible]** | | **(57)** |
| **Nationality** | | **(58)** |
| **Marital status, when moving** | | **(59)** |
| **Dependents, when moving** | | **(60)** |
| **Relatives in plant moved from** | | **(61)** |
| **Relatives in plant moved to** | | **(62)** |
| **Home and location of companies** | | **(63)** |

In addition to this information secured directly from the company records, we interviewed 233 of a sample of 270 workers,[1] most of whom had moved between two or more of the 37 firms. Effective contact with the others was impossible because they had moved from the region, had died, could not be located, or refused to be interviewed. In some of these cases, however, enough information was secured from friends or relatives to throw some light on the person's experience.

A copy of the form used by the interviewers is reproduced as Chart III. The approach used, however, was definitely informal, with the result that some of the questions on the form were occasionally unanswered and in many cases additional information not specified was secured. No mention was made by the interviewer of the fact that much of the worker's experience was already known from his previous or present employers' records. Instead, an effort was made to get the worker to talk as freely as possible, recounting his entire work experience as he remembered it or chose to tell it. There was no attempt to correct erroneous statements when they were made, and consequently the work histories as recorded on the interview forms were sometimes at variance with those portions of the worker's experience which were shown on the employers' records.[2]

These variations or discrepancies were analyzed in detail. The most common type of discrepancy was between the number of

[1] The interview sample was selected on a partly random basis. The 1,539 workers who moved between the 37 firms were divided into two groups: those who were still working at the last firm and those who had disappeared from the records after moving to the last firm. Since we were particularly interested in tracing the unemployment benefit experience of workers to be interviewed, the selection was confined largely to the second group — those who had disappeared from the records after moving from one firm to another. A random sample of 230 of these workers was taken, and 40 more were added to the interview group on a similar basis of selection from the employees who had worked only part of the period for only one of the 37 firms. The size of the sample was confined to this number in order that individual interviews could be obtained during the summer of 1940.

[2] Cf. Gladys L. Palmer, "The Reliability of Response in Labor Market Inquiries," Bureau of the Budget, Division of Statistical Standards, July, 1942.

CHART III

Name ______ Last address ______

Usual occupation ______ Date interviewed ______

**WORK HISTORY**

| Y | 1 Place of Employment | 2 How You Got the Job | 3 Dates | 4 Approx. Hourly Wage or Weekly Earn'gs | 5 Type of Job | 6 Experience | 7 Reasons for Leaving | 8 Unemployment Benefit and Relief History |
|---|---|---|---|---|---|---|---|---|
| 1937 | | | | | | | | |
| | | | | | | | | |
| 1938 | | | | | | | | |
| | | | | | | | | |
| 1939 | | | | | | | | |
| | | | | | | | | |

1. Do you want full-time work through the year? Yes No
   Part-time work? Yes No
   Seasonal work? Yes No
   Any other time?
2. Does your pay help support anyone else in your family? Yes No
   *a.* If not, do you keep it all for yourself? Yes No
   *b.* If not, are you normally supported by someone else in the family? Yes No
3. Does anyone else in your family work? Yes No
   (List their names and places of employment in the last three years.)

4. If you live in ______, have you ever worked in ______? Yes No
   If you live in ______, have you ever worked in ______? Yes No
   If so, where and when?
5. Have you ever worked outside ______ and ______? Yes No
   If so, where and when?
   Why did you come here?
6. Have you done farm work in the last three years? Yes No
   If so, did you receive pay, part of the crop, or sell some of your own garden crops?
7. If you received unemployment benefits or relief (including WPA), did you have any difficulty in getting them? Yes No
8. Did your unemployment benefits run out? Yes No
   If so, what did you do then?

jobs which the worker said he had held and the number which he actually had held during this period according to the employment records kept by various firms. More than a third of the 233 persons interviewed did not mention jobs which they were known to have had. The failure to mention one job was, of course, most frequent, but nineteen had forgotten or deliberately did not mention at least two jobs, and one person did not list seven of the jobs that were on his work history. It is significant to note that twenty of these "forgotten" jobs were in one company – a leather products concern which had one of the highest labor turnover figures of any in the group of thirty-seven.

A further clue as to why workers forgot some of their past jobs is found in the fact that more than half the jobs had lasted less than a month, and most of them were shorter than three months. It was seldom that a job held as long as six months was not mentioned by the worker at the interview. For this reason, we are inclined to attribute these omissions to "poor memory" rather than to a deliberate effort to conceal something from the interviewer. The latter was undoubtedly present in some cases, particularly in connection with questions on unemployment compensation, when the worker may have had the impression that an "investigation" was being made of his record. But its effect in connection with most of the other questions was probably slight.

Another discrepancy was found between the dates of jobs as given by the worker at the interview and the dates as shown on the company's records. Although there was a slight tendency to place jobs earlier than they actually were, workers were just about as likely to think that they had worked more recently for a firm than was actually the case. Similarly, there were errors in estimating the length of particular jobs, and workers tended to overestimate rather than underestimate the lengths of the jobs they had held in the preceding three years.

Exact reasons for leaving employment were not always available from the interviews and firm records for the same job. Where a direct comparison was possible, however, the reasons were the same in more than two-thirds of the cases. In those instances where workers gave a different reason at the interview from that recorded on the firm's employment records, the reason given by the worker was frequently more favorable than the recorded reason. For example, nine workers said they had been "laid off" from a particular job, whereas the firm's record showed that they had been discharged because they were "unsatisfactory." Six said they had "quit," but the records showed that they had been "laid off."

Finally, a frequent discrepancy was found between the size of the weekly paycheck which the worker claimed to have earned and the amount which his employment records showed he had actually earned. In those cases where a comparison was possible, more than five times as many workers overestimated their earnings as underestimated them. Usually the difference was small, but the tendency was nonetheless important.

One conclusion that stands out from this analysis of discrepancies between interviews and firm records is that workers' memories or statements cannot be relied upon for detailed factual information concerning their work experience. They are frequently unable to remember all the jobs they have had, the order in which they had them, the dates of employment, the length of their jobs, and their earnings. They occasionally give a different reason for leaving a job than that recorded by the firm, but this is explained largely in terms of a desire to cover up an unfavorable record rather than in terms of poor memory.

# Appendix B

## SUPPLEMENTARY TABLES AND CHARTS

TABLE 1

DISTRIBUTION OF TOTAL EMPLOYMENT, IN THE COMMUNITY STUDIED

(1930 Census) *

| Occupation | Male | Female | Total | Per Cent |
|---|---|---|---|---|
| Manufacturing and mechanical | 11,084 | 3,220 | 14,304 | 56 |
| Trade | 2,501 | 629 | 3,130 | 12 |
| Domestic and personal service | 719 | 1,411 | 2,130 | 8 |
| Transportation and communication | 1,738 | 136 | 1,874 | 7 |
| Professional service | 708 | 1,004 | 1,712 | 7 |
| Public service | 476 | 11 | 487 | 2 |
| Agriculture | 515 | 26 | 541 | 2 |
| Other † | 791 | 808 | 1,599 | 6 |
| Total | 18,532 | 7,245 | 25,777 | 100 |

* U. S. Census of Population, Vol. III, Part I, 1930, p. 1103. Separate tabulations were published for only one of the two cities, but a special tabulation for the other was made for *New England Community Statistical Abstracts* (Social and Economic Data for 175 New England Cities and Towns Prepared for the Industrial Development Committee of the New England Council), complied by Ralph G. Wells and John S. Perkins, Boston: Bureau of Better Business Research, Boston University, October, 1939. Table 1 above is a compilation from these sources.

† Includes clerical occupations which are listed separately for only one city.

TABLE 2

HALF-YEAR IN WHICH MOVEMENT TOOK PLACE

(In percentages, by types of movement)

| | Types of Movement (Reasons for Leaving) | 1937 | | 1938 | | 1939 | |
|---|---|---|---|---|---|---|---|
| | | 1st half | 2nd half | 1st half | 2nd half | 1st half | 2nd half |
| VOLUNTARY | Dissatisfaction with wages, hours, or working conditions | 4 | 3 | 3 | 1 | 1 | 1 |
| | More attractive opportunities elsewhere | 11 | 6 | 4 | 7 | 3 | 4 |
| | Community, family, personal, or physical reasons | 5 | 4 | 4 | 3 | 4 | 5 |
| | Miscellaneous (to retire,* to return to school, etc.) | 0 | † | 0 | † | † | 1 |
| | Voluntary but no further information given | 3 | 4 | 1 | 1 | 3 | 2 |
| | Sub-total, voluntary | 23 | 17 | 12 | 12 | 11 | 13 |
| FORCED | Discharged | 3 | 4 | 5 | 3 | 6 | 1 |
| | Laid off | 19 | 23 | 38 | 36 | 36 | 35 |
| | Sub-total, forced | 22 | 27 | 43 | 39 | 42 | 36 |
| | Reason for leaving unstated | 55 | 56 | 45 | 49 | 47 | 51 |
| | Total | 100 | 100 | 100 | 100 | 100 | 100 |

* Those who were listed as leaving "to retire" may have either changed their minds, left for another reason, or gone to another company that had a higher retirement age.

† Less than 1 per cent.

TABLE 3

DETAILED LIST OF REASONS FOR LEAVING LAST JOB

|  | | |
|---|---|---|
| I. Dissatisfaction with Wages, Hours, or Working Conditions . . | | 52 |
| *A.* Dissatisfaction with wages (general) | 7 | |
| 1. Dissatisfaction with wage rate | 1 | |
| 2. Dissatisfaction with weekly earnings | 6 | |
| 3. Dissatisfaction with method of pay | 1 | |
| Sub-total | 15 | |
| *B.* Dissatisfaction with nature of job or working conditions | 6 | |
| 1. Work too hard or heavy | 8 | |
| 2. Work causes too much nerve strain | 4 | |
| 3. Work causes too much eye strain | 2 | |
| 4. Work unhealthful | 1 | |
| 5. Dissatisfaction with new machine | 1 | |
| Sub-total | 22 | |
| *C.* Dissatisfaction with hours or time of work | 0 | |
| 1. Night work | 2 | |
| 2. No work or not enough work | 6 | |
| Sub-total | 8 | |
| *D.* Dissatisfaction with labor policies | 0 | |
| 1. Dislike of foreman | 4 | |
| 2. Unadjusted grievance | 1 | |
| 3. Strike | 1 | |
| 4. Desire for vacation or change of work | 1 | |
| Sub-total | 7 | |
| II. More Attractive Opportunities Elsewhere . . . . . . | | 140 |
| *A.* To take another job | 57 | |
| *B.* To better myself | 14 | |
| *C.* To take job with better future | 2 | |
| *D.* To take former job | 50 | |
| *E.* To take steadier work | 17 | |
| III. Community, Family, Personal, or Physical Reasons . . . . | | 96 |
| *A.* Community and family reasons | | |
| 1. Sickness in family | 4 | |
| 2. Needed at home | 15 | |
| Sub-total | 19 | |
| *B.* Personal reasons | | |
| 1. To accompany friend leaving | 1 | |
| 2. Leaving city | 2 | |
| 3. So husband can get job | 1 | |
| 4. Failed to return after leave of absence | 4 | |
| 5. Leave of absence | 4 | |
| Sub-total | 12 | |

TABLE 3 (*continued*)

| Reason | Sub-item | Total |
|---|---|---|
| *C.* Physical reasons | | |
| 1. Superannuated | 1 | |
| 2. Ill health due to factory work | 2 | |
| 3. Ill health | 55 | |
| 4. Injury from work | 2 | |
| 5. Pregnancy | 5 | |
| Sub-total | 65 | |
| IV. Miscellaneous Voluntary | | 6 |
| *A.* To retire | 3 | |
| *B.* To go to school | 3 | |
| V. Voluntary — No Further Explanation | | 55 |
| *A.* Resigned or left voluntarily | 40 | |
| *B.* Left without final interview | 1 | |
| *C.* Left without notice or failed to report | 13 | |
| *D.* Hired but failed to report | 1 | |
| VI. Discharged | | 90 |
| *A.* For incompetency | | |
| 1. Not satisfactory | 49 | |
| 2. Worker is slow | 6 | |
| 3. Physically unadapted | 4 | |
| 4. Incompetent | 11 | |
| 5. Spoiling work | 1 | |
| Sub-total | 71 | |
| *B.* For disciplinary reasons | | |
| 1. Misconduct | 2 | |
| 2. Habitually absent | 4 | |
| 3. Unreliable | 2 | |
| 4. Dissatisfied | 1 | |
| 5. Disturber or trouble maker | 2 | |
| 6. Violation of rules | 1 | |
| 7. Insubordination | 3 | |
| 8. Dishonesty | 4 | |
| Sub-total | 19 | |
| VII. Laid Off | | 784 |
| *A.* Business conditions | 750 | |
| 1. Completion of temporary work | 18 | |
| Sub-total | 768 | |
| *B.* Manufacturing conditions | | |
| 1. Change in industrial process | 1 | |
| 2. Discontinuance of department | 7 | |
| 3. Shortage of material | 3 | |
| 4. Breakdown | 3 | |
| 5. Strike or lockout | 1 | |
| 6. No machine available | 1 | |
| Sub-total | 16 | |
| VIII. Reason for Leaving Unknown | | 1,228 |
| Total all reasons | | 2,451 |

TABLE 4

PERSONS MOVING CLASSIFIED ACCORDING TO WHETHER OR NOT THEY HAD WORKED BEFORE IN FIRM MOVED TO

| | Reason for leaving | Yes | | No | | Total |
|---|---|---|---|---|---|---|
| | | Number | Per Cent | Number | Per Cent | |
| VOLUNTARY | Dissatisfied | 13 | 25 | 39 | 75 | 52 |
| | Better job | 66 | 47 | 74 | 53 | 140 |
| | Family, personal | 22 | 23 | 74 | 77 | 96 |
| | Miscellaneous | 0 | 0 | 6 | 100 | 6 |
| | No details | 14 | 25 | 41 | 75 | 55 |
| | Sub-total | 115 | 33 | 234 | 67 | 349 |
| FORCED | Discharged | 17 | 19 | 73 | 81 | 90 |
| | Laid off | 181 | 23 | 603 | 77 | 784 |
| | Sub-total | 198 | 23 | 676 | 77 | 874 |
| | Unknown | 324 | 26 | 904 | 74 | 1,228 |
| | Total | 637 | 26 | 1,814 | 74 | 2,451 |

TABLE 5

SEASONALITY OF EMPLOYMENT

(Ranking of the 10 Industries in the Sample)*

| Rank | Industry | Index of Variation† |
|---|---|---|
| 1 | Shoes and leather products | 156.1 |
| 2 | Plastics | 115.5 |
| 3 | Furniture | 106.5 |
| 4 | Machinery | 100.6‡ |
| 5 | Textiles | 91.3 |
| 6 | Converted paper products | 78.4 |
| 7 | Apparel | 53.0 |
| 8 | Metal products | 26.0 |
| 9 | Public utilities | 22.2 |
| 10 | Paper manufacturing | 13.8 |

* "Food Products" was omitted because only one firm was included in the sample.

† The original data for this index were the number of wage earners in the firms by months. From these data a seasonal index, by months, was calculated on the basis of a 12 months' moving average centered at the middle of the month. The sum of the absolute deviations of this index from 100 was used as a measure of variability of the employment of the firm. The industry measure was constructed by weighting the firm measures by the average monthly employment of the firm for the whole period (1937–39) and taking an arithmetic average.

‡ The fluctuation in the machinery industry was due more to completion of special orders, and to shutdowns for repairs, than to seasonal variations in the demand for the product.

TABLE 6

LABOR MARKET CALENDAR

Peak Months in Neighboring Seasonal Industries

| | Plastics Neighborhood | | | Shoes–Cotton Textile Neighborhood | | |
|---|---|---|---|---|---|---|
| January | | | | | | Metal products* (slight peak) |
| February | | | | Shoes | | Metal products (slight peak) |
| March | | Apparel | Converted paper products | Shoes | Cotton textiles | |
| April | Plastics | Apparel | Furniture | Shoes | Cotton textiles | |
| May | Plastics | | | | Cotton textiles | |
| June | | | | | | |
| July | | | | | | |
| August | Plastics | | Furniture | | Cotton textiles | |
| September | Plastics | Apparel | Furniture | Shoes | Cotton textiles | |
| October | Plastics | Apparel | Furniture<br>Converted paper products | Shoes | | |
| November | | Apparel | Furniture<br>Converted paper products | Shoes | | |
| December | | Apparel | | | | |

* Metal products was not one of the more seasonal industries, but there was a slight peak in the first part of each year.

TABLE 7

INTERINDUSTRY AND INTRAINDUSTRY MOVEMENT

| Number of moves to firms in | Number of Moves from Firms in | | | | | | | | | | | |
|---|---|---|---|---|---|---|---|---|---|---|---|---|
| | Plastics | Apparel | Furniture | Converted Paper Products | Shoes and Leather Products | Textiles | Metal Products | Paper Manufacturing | Machinery | Public Utilities | Food Products | Total |
| Plastics | 913 | 126 | 86 | 47 | 31 | 30 | 8 | 0 | 3 | 0 | 0 | 1,244 |
| Apparel | 153 | 95 | 20 | 5 | 5 | 3 | 0 | 0 | 1 | 0 | 0 | 282 |
| Furniture | 76 | 13 | 27 | 17 | 5 | 11 | 4 | 0 | 1 | 0 | 0 | 154 |
| Converted paper products | 48 | 6 | 15 | 3 | 2 | 2 | 1 | 1 | 0 | 0 | 0 | 78 |
| Shoes and leather products | 15 | 7 | 3 | 0 | 103 | 36 | 23 | 5 | 0 | 0 | 1 | 193 |
| Textiles | 19 | 1 | 7 | 3 | 53 | 174 | 18 | 6 | 1 | 0 | 4 | 286 |
| Metal products | 5 | 1 | 3 | 0 | 29 | 12 | 8 | 6 | 3 | 1 | 0 | 68 |
| Paper manufacturing | 1 | 1 | 5 | 0 | 20 | 28 | 22 | 5 | 3 | 3 | 2 | 90 |
| Machinery | 10 | 3 | 3 | 0 | 3 | 1 | 8 | 0 | 11 | 1 | 0 | 40 |
| Public utilities | 0 | 0 | 1 | 0 | 0 | 4 | 5 | 2 | 0 | 2 | 0 | 14 |
| Food products | 0 | 0 | 0 | 0 | 1 | 1 | 0 | 0 | 0 | 0 | 0 | 2 |
| Total | 1,240 | 253 | 170 | 75 | 252 | 302 | 97 | 25 | 23 | 7 | 7 | 2,451 |

TABLE 8

WEEKS WORKED BEFORE MOVING VOLUNTARILY*

| Weeks | Number | Per Cent | Cumulative Per Cent |
|---|---|---|---|
| 0–4 | 52 | 33 | 34 |
| 5–9 | 26 | 16 | 49 |
| 10–14 | 12 | 8 | 57 |
| 15–19 | 19 | 12 | 69 |
| 20–24 | 9 | 6 | 75 |
| 25–29 | 9 | 6 | 80 |
| 30–34 | 3 | 2 | 83 |
| 35–39 | 4 | 2 | 85 |
| 40–44 | 1 | 1 | 86 |
| 45–49 | 3 | 2 | 88 |
| Over 50 | 14 | 9 | 97 |
| Not stated | 5 | 3 | 100 |
| Total | 157 | 100 | |

* In this table only those workers who moved voluntarily because of dissatisfaction with wages or earnings, better opportunities elsewhere, or to return to a former job are included in the group of " workers moving voluntarily."

TABLE 9

PERSONNEL CHARACTERISTICS OF ALL WORKERS WHO MOVED VOLUNTARILY

(Compared with Those in the Voluntary Group Who Stayed Less than 30 Weeks at the Firm to Which They Moved)

| Personnel Characteristics | | Workers Moving Voluntarily | | Workers in Voluntary Group Who Stayed Less than 30 Weeks at Firm to Which They Moved* | |
|---|---|---|---|---|---|
| | | Number | Per Cent | Number | Per Cent |
| Age | Under 25 | 171 | 49 | 28 | 58 |
| | 25–34 | 93 | 27 | 17 | 36 |
| | 35–44 | 60 | 17 | 3 | 6 |
| | 45 and over | 22 | 6 | 0 | 0 |
| | Unknown | 3 | 1 | 0 | 0 |
| Sex | Male | 85 | 24 | 18 | 37 |
| | Female | 264 | 76 | 30 | 63 |
| Marital Status | Single | 136 | 39 | 27 | 57 |
| | Married | 197 | 56 | 16 | 33 |
| | Widowed or divorced | 7 | 2 | 1 | 2 |
| | Unknown | 9 | 3 | 4 | 8 |

* This group includes only those who moved voluntarily because of dissatisfaction with wages or earnings or because of the prospect of a better job. It is this group which provides the significant comparison with all the workers who moved voluntarily.

TABLE 10

AVERAGE HOURLY AND WEEKLY EARNINGS OF WORKERS WHO MOVED VOLUNTARILY

(Compared with a Sample of Workers Continuously Employed, 1937–39, at Any One of the 10 Firms with Most Voluntary Movement)*

| | | Workers Moving Voluntarily | | Workers Continuously Employed at One Firm | |
|---|---|---|---|---|---|
| | | Number | Per Cent | Number | Per Cent |
| HOURLY | Under 20¢ | 11 | 7 | 1 | 3 |
| | 20–29¢ | 39 | 25 | 0 | 0 |
| | 30–39¢ | 55 | 35 | 6 | 17 |
| | 40–49¢ | 31 | 20 | 9 | 28 |
| | 50–59¢ | 7 | 4 | 11 | 32 |
| | 60¢ or over | 9 | 6 | 5 | 14 |
| | Unknown | 5 | 3 | 2 | 6 |
| | Total | 157 | 100 | 34 | 100 |
| WEEKLY | Under $5.00 | 12 | 8 | 0 | 0 |
| | $5.00–$9.99 | 42 | 27 | 0 | 0 |
| | $10.00–$14.99 | 55 | 35 | 10 | 29 |
| | $15.00–$19.99 | 21 | 13 | 14 | 41 |
| | $20.00–$24.99 | 8 | 5 | 4 | 12 |
| | $25.00 or over | 7 | 4 | 5 | 15 |
| | Unknown | 12 | 8 | 1 | 3 |
| | Total | 157 | 100 | 34 | 100 |

* The sample of continuously employed workers is identical with that in Table 5, but in this table only those workers who moved voluntarily because of dissatisfaction with wages or earnings, better opportunities elsewhere, or to return to a former job are included in the group of "workers moving voluntarily." The average hourly and average weekly earnings figures for this group cover the last 6-months' period of employment in the firm moved from. For the continuously employed sample the figures apply to 1937 only.

TABLE 11

AVERAGE NUMBER OF WEEKS WORKED AT LAST FIRM BEFORE LEAVING

| Rank | Mean Average Weeks Worked | | Median Average Weeks Worked | |
|---|---|---|---|---|
| 1 | Laid off | (24 wks.) | Laid off | (14 wks.) |
| 2 | Better job | (21 wks.) | Dissatisfied | (12 wks.) |
| 3 | Miscellaneous — voluntary | (20 wks.) | Better job | (11 wks.) |
| 4 | Unknown | (18 wks.) | Voluntary — no details | (9 wks.) |
| 5 | Dissatisfied | (18 wks.) | Unknown | (9 wks.) |
| 6 | Family, personal | (16 wks.) | Miscellaneous — voluntary | (8 wks.) |
| 7 | Discharged | (15 wks.) | Family, personal | (7 wks.) |
| 8 | Voluntary — no details | (14 wks.) | Discharged | (6 wks.) |
| All movements | | (20 wks.) | | |

TABLE 12

PERSONNEL CHARACTERISTICS OF WORKERS WHO WERE DISCHARGED

(Compared with a Sample of Workers Continuously Employed, 1937–39, at Any One of the 10 Firms with the Most Forced Movements Due to Discharges) *

| | | Workers Discharged (in Moving Groups) | | Workers Continuously Employed in One Firm | |
|---|---|---|---|---|---|
| | | Number | Per Cent | Number | Per Cent |
| Age | Under 25 | 63 | 70 | 8 | 20 |
| | 25–34 | 14 | 15 | 18 | 44 |
| | 35–44 | 6 | 7 | 6 | 15 |
| | 45 and over | 7 | 8 | 8 | 20 |
| | Unknown | 0 | 0 | 1 | 3 |
| Sex | Male | 30 | 33 | 22 | 54 |
| | Female | 60 | 67 | 19 | 46 |
| Marital status | Single | 56 | 62 | 17 | 42 |
| | Married | 31 | 35 | 23 | 56 |
| | Widowed or divorced | 1 | 1 | 1 | 2 |
| | Unknown | 2 | 2 | 0 | 0 |
| Nationality | Native American | 21 | 23 | 13 | 32 |
| | French-Canadian | 32 | 36 | 13 | 32 |
| | Italian | 17 | 19 | 10 | 24 |
| | Irish | 6 | 7 | 0 | 0 |
| | Finnish | 2 | 2 | 1 | 2 |
| | Other Nationality | 8 | 9 | 4 | 10 |
| | Unknown | 4 | 4 | 0 | 0 |

* This "continuously employed" sample was selected at random, one in fifty, from the 2,014 continuously employed workers in the 10 firms which had the most forced movement due to discharges.

TABLE 13

DIFFERENCE IN AVERAGE HOURLY EARNINGS AT THE TWO FIRMS BETWEEN WHICH MOVEMENT OCCURRED*

| Cents per Hour Difference | Reasons for Leaving | | | | | |
|---|---|---|---|---|---|---|
| | Dissatisfaction with Wages and Earnings | Per Cent | Better Job | Per Cent | To Return to Former Job | Per Cent |
| Total who got more (after moving) | 10 | 48 | 46 | 54 | 31 | 62 |
| 25¢ (and over) more | 0 | 0 | 3 | 3 | 1 | 2 |
| 21–24¢ more | 0 | 0 | 1 | 1 | 4 | 8 |
| 17–20¢ more | 0 | 0 | 6 | 7 | 5 | 10 |
| 13–16¢ more | 0 | 0 | 4 | 5 | 3 | 6 |
| 9–12¢ more | 6 | 29 | 11 | 13 | 5 | 10 |
| 5–8¢ more | 3 | 14 | 12 | 14 | 6 | 12 |
| 1–4¢ more | 1 | 5 | 9 | 11 | 7 | 14 |
| No change | 2 | 9 | 9 | 11 | 3 | 6 |
| 1–4¢ less | 0 | 0 | 4 | 5 | 1 | 2 |
| 5–8¢ less | 4 | 19 | 7 | 9 | 5 | 10 |
| 9–12¢ less | 0 | 0 | 6 | 7 | 0 | 0 |
| 13–16¢ less | 0 | 0 | 2 | 2 | 1 | 2 |
| 17–20¢ less | 0 | 0 | 3 | 3 | 0 | 0 |
| 21–24¢ less | 0 | 0 | 1 | 1 | 0 | 0 |
| 25¢ (and over) less | 0 | 0 | 2 | 2 | 1 | 2 |
| Total who got less | 4 | 19 | 25 | 29 | 8 | 16 |
| Not given | 5 | 24 | 5 | 6 | 8 | 16 |
| Total | 21 | 100 | 85 | 100 | 50 | 100 |

* First 6 months' average hourly earnings at firm moved to compared to last 6 months' average hourly earnings at plant moved from, based on the former.

The totals in this and the following tables do not correspond to the totals on which Table 2 is based because only selected voluntary reasons were included here. This was done to eliminate reasons unrelated to wages or earnings, such as "dissatisfaction with the foreman."

TABLE 14

AVERAGE HOURLY EARNINGS AT NEXT FIRM COMPARED TO LAST FIRM

| | Dissatisfaction with Wages, etc. | Better Job | To Return to Former Job | Total |
|---|---|---|---|---|
| Consistently higher | 3 | 16 | 18 | 37 |
| Beginning rates lower but higher after first 6 months | 2 | 5 | 2 | 9 |
| Beginning rates same but higher after first 6 months | 0 | 4 | 1 | 5 |
| No change | 1 | 5 | 4 | 10 |
| Lower | 1 | 6 | 4 | 11 |
| Not employed beyond first 6 months' period | 13 | 47 | 15 | 75 |
| Not given | 1 | 2 | 6 | 10 |
| Total | 21 | 85 | 50 | 157 |

TABLE 15

AVERAGE NUMBER OF MONTHS BETWEEN JOBS, RANKED ACCORDING TO TYPES OF MOVEMENT

| Rank | Mean Average Months | Median Average Months |
|---|---|---|
| 1 | Miscellaneous—voluntary (10.5 months) | Miscellaneous—voluntary (11.2 months) |
| 2 | Family, personal reasons (6.2 " ) | Family, personal reasons (4.1 " ) |
| 3 | Discharged (4.7 " ) | Discharged (2.7 " ) |
| 4 | Voluntary — No details (4.4 " ) | Laid off (2.4 " ) |
| 5 | Laid off (4.0 " ) | Voluntary — No details (1.9 " ) |
| 6 | Dissatisfied (3.9 " ) | Dissatisfied (1.2 " ) |
| 7 | Not given (3.9 " ) | Not given (1.2 " ) |
| 8 | Better job (1.2 " ) | Better job (0.1 " ) |

TABLE 16

AVERAGE HOURLY AND AVERAGE WEEKLY EARNINGS AT THE TWO FIRMS BETWEEN WHICH FORCED MOVEMENT OCCURRED*

| Reason for Leaving | | Earnings of Next Firm as Compared to Previous Firm | | | | Total |
|---|---|---|---|---|---|---|
| | | Higher | No Change | Lower | Unknown | |
| HOURLY | Discharged | 31 | 18 | 29 | 12 | 90 |
| | Laid off | 228 | 133 | 313 | 110 | 784 |
| | Sub-total | 259 | 151 | 342 | 122 | 874 |
| WEEKLY | Discharged | 32 | 20 | 26 | 12 | 90 |
| | Laid off | 251 | 136 | 287 | 110 | 784 |
| | Sub-total | 283 | 156 | 313 | 122 | 874 |

* Last 6 months' earnings at firm moved from as compared to first 6 months' earnings at firm to which movement occurred.

Chart IV

Manufacturing Employment in a Sample of Firms in this Labor Market, Massachusetts, and United States*

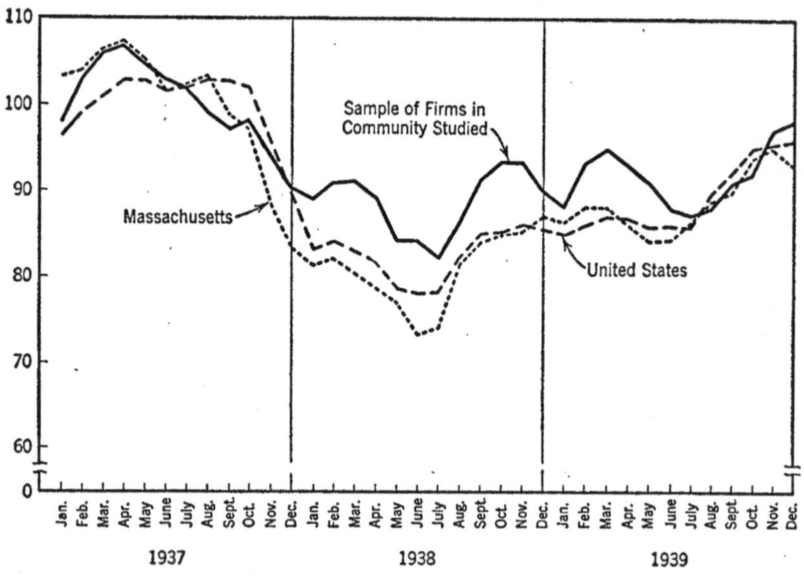


* The base in each series is the monthly average for 1937. Relatives were computed from data supplied by the Massachusetts Department of Labor and Industries for the sample of firms, with their permission. The 1940 Supplement of the *Survey of Current Business* is the source of the series for Massachusetts and the United States. These series are unadjusted for seasonal variation.

Chart V

The Relationship between the Wage Rate Level, Over-all Labor Turnover, and Worker Movement in 34 Firms* for 1937-39

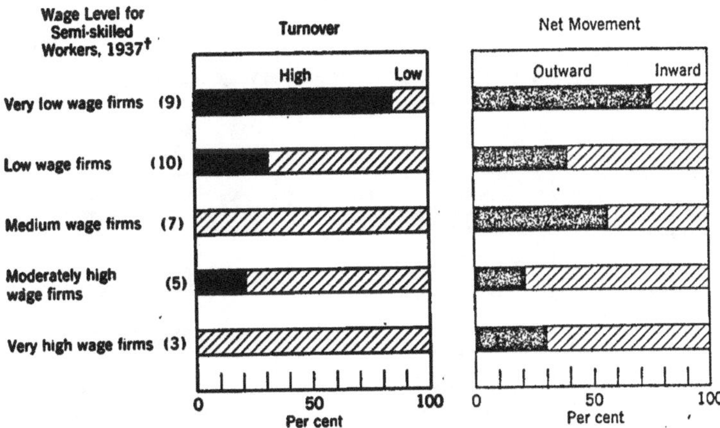


The Relationship between the Number of General Wage Increases Given by the Firms, Over-all Labor Turnover, and Worker Movement for 1937-39

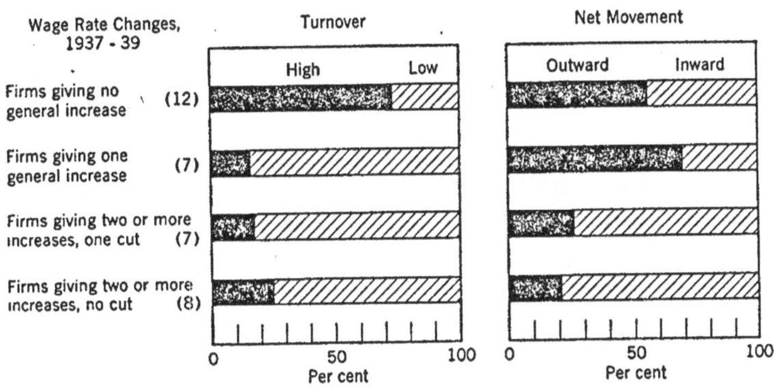


Percentage of firms with high over-all turnover (over 1.67) or net movement outward

Percentage of firms with low over-all turnover (under 1.67) or net movement inward

* The two public utility firms and one metal products firm are omitted from this analysis because of insufficient data for some of the comparisons. For a discussion of "over-all turnover" and "net movement," see page 55, note 1.

† Information on the approximate hourly wage rates or, if piece rates were paid, the straight time average hourly earnings for semi-skilled workers (such as assemblers or machine-operators), were supplied by each firm.

Chart VI

The Relationship between the Timing of General Wage Increases, Over-all Labor Turnover, and Worker Movement, for 1937-39

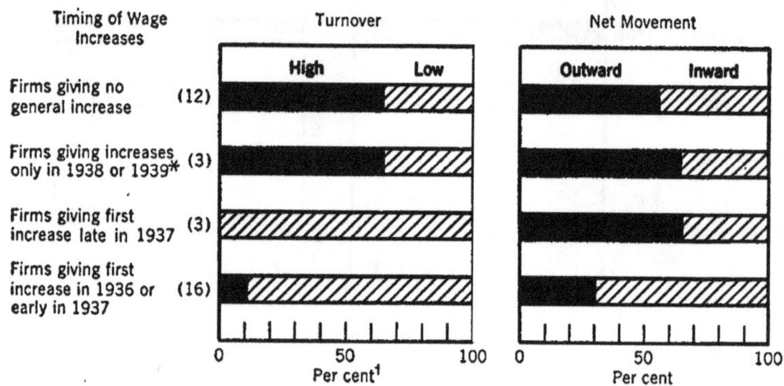


The Relationship between the Nature of the Firms' Welfare Plans, Over-all Labor Turnover, and Worker Movement, for 1937-39

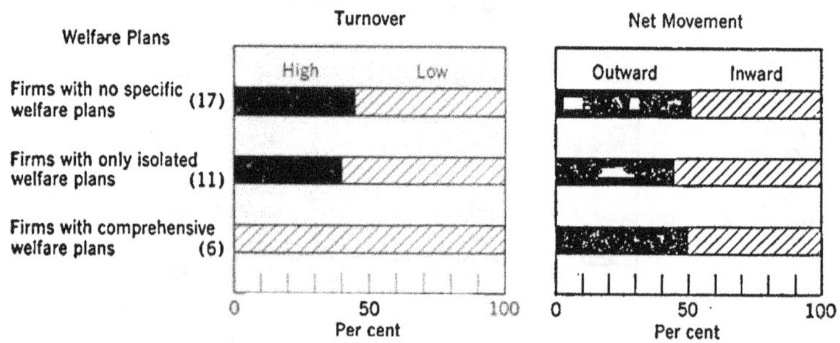


* As a result of reduction in hours under the FLSA, three firms increased their wage rates to maintain weekly earnings.

† Key for the diagrams is the same as the one in Chart V.

Chart VII

The Relationship between Informal Labor Relations Practices, Over-all Labor Turnover, and Worker Movement, for 1937-39

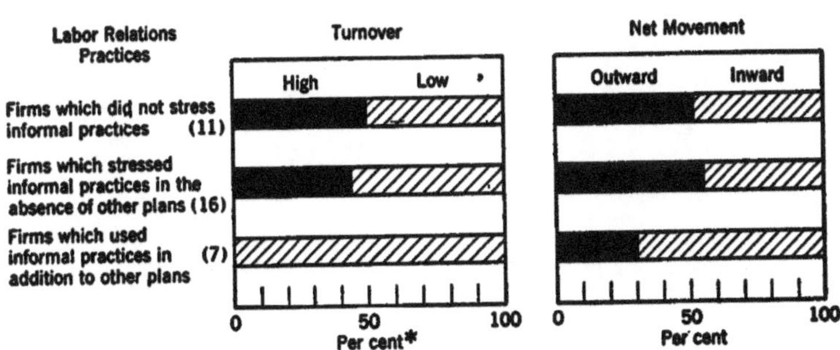


The Relationship between Working Conditions in the Firms, Over-all Labor Turnover, and Worker Movement, for 1937-39

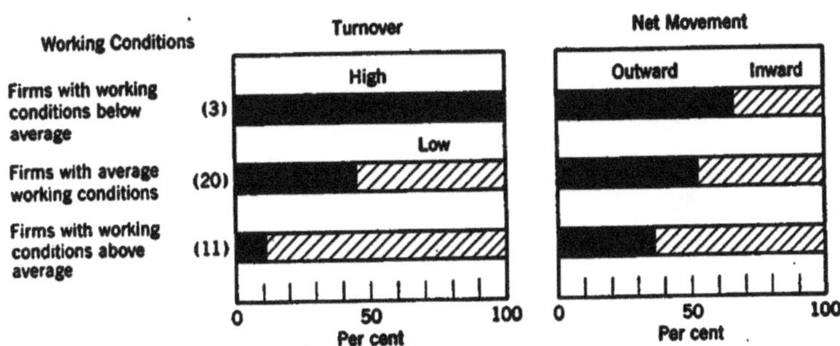


* The key for the diagrams is the same as in Chart V.

# INDEX

www.ingramcontent.com/pod-product-compliance
Lightning Source LLC
Chambersburg PA
CBHW031813190326
41518CB00006B/312

* 9 7 8 0 2 6 2 6 3 2 7 6 8 *